COMFORT PIE

COMFORT PIE

Kathryn Hawkins

Front Table Books
An Imprint of Cedar Fort, Inc.
Springville, Utah

First published in the United States by Cedar Fort Publishing & Media
Published in the United Kingdom by New Holland Publishers (UK) Ltd.

US edition published in 2013 by Front Table Books, an imprint of Cedar Fort, Inc.
2373 W. 700 S., Springville, UT, 84663
Distributed by Cedar Fort, Inc., www.cedarfort.com

ISBN 13: 978-1-4621-1292-0

LIBRARY OF CONGRESS CATALOGING-IN-PUBLICATION DATA ON FILE

Cover design by Erica Dixon
Cover design © 2013 by Lyle Mortimer
Editing for the US edition by Shelby Law

Printed in China

10 9 8 7 6 5 4 3 2 1

CONTENTS

The idea for this book came from a conversation I had with my
mum, so I'd like to dedicate the finished work to her
and thank her for her inspiration.

INTRODUCTION

Pie is something I can remember eating and enjoying throughout my childhood. Ground meat, sausage, or cheese and potato pies made inexpensive, tasty, and filling suppers for our mother to make us, and on the weekend, for a special treat, we would have a homemade apple pie with custard or sometimes vanilla ice cream—we didn't have a freezer, so we would wait in pie-eyed anticipation while Dad went off to the corner shop to buy an icy, cardboard-packed square of Cornish ice cream before we could eat. On every picnic, there was always a pie in some form or other—individual pork sausage rolls or a wedge of egg and bacon pie were the most memorable.

When we went on vacation to stay with my grandparents in Devon, Grannie Watts would always produce a homegrown fruit pie at some point—usually rhubarb or black currant—served with luscious clotted cream. And always with homemade, short, buttery pastry—there were no shortcuts in those days!—and a quirky blackbird pie funnel sticking out the top. Grannie's sister-in-law Dorothy used to bake for the family café, and a visit to see her on the way to the beach meant that our picnic basket would be embellished with freshly baked, and still warm, savory pasties.

I do remember bad pie experiences just as well, though: school dinner pies are certainly among the worst ones I have eaten. I can't remember anything savory, just the pudding ones. The pastry was dry, hard, and tasteless—mercifully only pastry on the bottom—and the filling or topping was either too sweet, paste-like and flavorless, or so sparse it looked like it had only been shown the pastry!

What is a pie? Well, I think a pie means different things to different people, so for the purposes of this book, I have kept to my own specific boundaries. First and most importantly, it must have pastry as the key ingredient—you'll find no mashed potato tops or other pastry-less pies in this book. Secondly, the pastry should be baked to form a crisp crust or shell—so no steamed pastry. And finally, my pies have either a pastry top and bottom (or all around pastry casing) or are top crust only—this is typically British; if there is bottom crust (like an American pie), it must support a good, hearty portion of filling and be topped in some way. Apart from that, they can be any shape or size, in or out of a tin or dish, and made up with any type of pastry.

Pastry is a vital constituent of a really good pie, but the filling is of equal importance. While I have been writing my recipes, quite by chance, I was asked to be a judge on a panel for the Perthshire region of the Scottish Association of Meat Traders Steak Pie and Speciality Pie Competition. I met some experienced pie making butchers who explained the techniques they used to get the right amount of filling in a dish but still achieve a good, crisp puff pastry layer on top. We had a fine time looking at the differing pastry textures and tasting the meat and gravy, and it was a very interesting and extremely timely experience for me. Overall, it was the pastry that let most pies down, and then seasoning came in a close second.

I have tried to come up with pies for every occasion in the recipe section. To start with, you'll find recipes for different types of pastry if you fancy making your own—if you have sufficient time, I do recommend you try. There is something very satisfying about making your own pastry, and the taste and texture of the baked result is far superior to anything readymade. However, time is of the essence, so I do state the quantity of pastry each recipe makes to enable you to substitute a readymade version if you need to.

There are 70 glorious pie recipes that follow the basic pastries, which are divided up into different chapters depending on the filling, and you'll find recipes for large family pies as well as individual ones, using a variety of different types of pastry.

Before you start cooking, though, you should read my tips and techniques on general pie and pastry making. Making a large, meat-filled pie is quite an investment of time and ingredients, so it seems a shame not to get a good result because of a simple problem in putting the pie together.

I hope you enjoy the book. I certainly had fun making all the pies and sharing them with friends and family, watching faces light up as I produced my latest pastry creation. Pies are a very sociable food, and everyone seems to appreciate a good one.

Happy pie making!

Kathryn

A BRIEF HISTORY OF PIES

Pies are recognized and baked all over the world in many shapes, forms, and sizes, but many languages offer no exact translation of the word; this leads food historians to believe that pies evolved in Europe, especially in northern regions. When I first came to write on the subject, every book I owned on the subject of British food history was littered with references to pies dating back to medieval times, but in other books of global culinary history, they occured only as introduced dishes. In *Larousse Gastronomique,* under the entry for "pie," I read: "The French have adopted the word for the classic British and American pies." I like to deduce from my research, therefore, that the pie is a very British dish, which we have shared with our cousins across the Atlantic Ocean! Pies are also popular in Australia and New Zealand.

Pies of old were primarily a means to cook, keep, and transport an assortment of fillings—the tough dough casing was never eaten. It is thought that the word pie ("pâté" in Medieval English) has an ornithological derivation and comes from magpie—a bird with the habit of collecting things. As with many familiar things, of the many historical references throughout culinary history, pies can also be dated back to the Egyptians.

"Humble pie" dates back to medieval times. Now a common saying, it evolved in households where the people at the top of the pecking order would get the prime cuts and the poor workers would get a pie full of entrails and offal—you'll find my version of this recipe inside this book. Cornish tin miners used to carry a pastry with savory mixture at one end and fruit or jam at the other in a roughly honed dough which was discarded once the insides were eaten—this was the original Cornish pasty. It was during the times of the Tudors that pastry, or "paste" as it was known then, really became part of the dish called "pie". Eggs were added as well as cold fats like butter and suet, and a more refined wheat flour was used for baking. Standing pies, like our raised pies of today, sound truly magnificent—like pieces of art you could actually eat. Pastry animals, birds, leaves, and foliage were embossed or stuck all over the outside—just like we do today with our (crude in comparison) pastry cutters, and the patterns on the outside often depicted the filling within. For banquets and feasts, heraldic emblems, coats of arms, and other family emblems were also used as edible decor.

Shortcrust pastry recipes were recorded as early as 1545, but it wasn't for another 50 years or so that flakier recipes started to appear written down. I've often wondered how puff pastry was first discovered—did someone forget to add the fat to the dough and then try to incorporate it afterwards?

Flaky pastry was an Arabic invention around 1500. At the same time, the Turkish were making filo ("phyllo" meaning leaf) sheet pastries for savory and sweet dishes, and their rule over parts of Eastern Europe meant that this pastry was adapted by the Hungarians and Austrians to make their strudels.

By the end of the sixteenth century, pastry was widely made and eaten all over the world. The first American pie recipes began to appear in the late eighteenth century, when fat was rubbed into the flour for a fine texture and some rolled in to give a good flaky crust. American pies are usually bottom crust only, which the British often refer to as a tart. Rarely have pies gone out of fashion, and with our renewed enthusiasm for baking, comfort food, and getting back in the kitchen, we're all cooking like never before, and pies are everywhere!

THE BASICS OF PASTRY MAKING

There is no real mystery to producing a good pie, but there are a few basics that you need to understand before you get started. Even if you're using a readymade pastry, you'll still get a better result if you follow the same guidelines. I don't think you can rush a pie and expect it to look or taste good. I think a pie is an impressive beast whatever the occasion, and it seems a shame to rush it and then have it not turn out to your best advantage. A pie is a real labor of love, and whoever you're serving it to will love you all the more for taking the time to get it tasting and looking right. With this in mind, I've put together some tips and techniques as well as my basic "pie rules" and general information to help you achieve your perfect, homely, satisfying, and deliciously perfect pie. Read on, pie enthusiasts.

Pastry Ingredients

1) FLOUR

Flour provides the main bulk and structure of any pastry. Wheat flour contains proteins, which form gluten, and gluten helps the pastry firm up and crisp when baked. All purpose or plain white wheat flour is the most commonly used for a standard shortcrust pastry, with the whole wheat (brown) version offering a healthier, more wholesome crust. Wheat flour with added rising agent (self-rising flour) is used for a softer textured pastry like suet crust, but if you enjoy experimenting, it can be used for shortcrust and will make a crumbly textured pastry which merges into the filling during baking and offers a less pronounced crust.

If you are wheat intolerant, you can use gluten-free flours—I have included suggestions and recipes. Pastry made with a gluten-free flour will have a different texture but can still provide a perfectly adequate casing for many different fillings. Remember to choose a flour that will combine well with filling flavors. For example, some flours, like chickpea (gram) have a beany, earthy flavor and are best suited to savory fillings.

For pastries with layers and flakes (flaky, rough puff, or puff) or when a more robust or free-standing pastry case is required (hot water crust), a wheat flour with a higher protein content and thus more gluten is often used. Choose bread (strong plain) or white bread flour for a firmer, crisper result. However, a bread flour with too high a protein content can make a tough pastry that shrinks. All purpose (plain) flour can be used for these pastries too, and the results will be slightly softer and flakier in texture; the type you choose is up to personal experimentation and taste.

As with all pastry ingredients, make sure you use fresh flour for best results. Store flours in bags, well-sealed, in a cool, dry place.

2) Fat

Fat determines the texture and flavor of a pastry. Butter, vegetable shortening, and lard are the most commonly used, but vegetable oils can also be used. Weigh or measure fat carefully, as too much can make the pastry greasy and short (difficult to handle), while not enough will make a hard, dry pastry. Usually, lard and butter are used together for best results; the former gives a short, crisp texture while the latter adds flavor. You will see recipes using combinations or a single fat. Choosing a hard vegetable fat is up to personal taste and health preferences. Choose an unsalted fat or one with with a low salt content so that you can control the seasoning of the pastry—see notes on salt below. Avoid low-fat spreads or any fat with an added water content ("spreadable"); they will alter the texture of the finished pastry.

Shredded beef or vegetable suet is used for suet crust pastries. It's up to personal taste which you prefer to use; personally, I prefer beef suet with savory fillings and vegetable suet with sweet fillings or delicate flavors like vegetables, fish, and poultry.

If you want to experiment with different oils, make sure you choose an oil that is suitable for cooking. Delicate flavored oils such as extra virgin olive or nut oils are not heat-resistant—they are used to flavor a finished dish rather than to cook with. However, when they are blended with a more robust oil like sunflower, they can be used for flavoring purposes in cooking. Remember that the color and flavor of an oil will affect the final taste of the pie, so it is worth choosing a blander-flavored vegetable oil if you don't want the pastry to dominate the pie filling.

Try to get the fat at the right temperature before blending with your flour. Rock-hard fat, straight from the fridge, is too difficult to blend, but if it is too soft, the fat has already started to melt and won't combine with the flour correctly. Don't be tempted to heat fat in the microwave in order to soften it in a hurry; more than likely, it will get too soft and will ruin the pastry. Ideally, take the fat out of the fridge about 30 minutes before using it to make sure the fat is firm and cool, not soft and oily.

3) Liquids

Water is the most commonly used liquid in pastry making and acts as a binding agent, bringing the flour and fat together to make a dough. In general, 1 teaspoon of cold water is used per 2 tablespoons (25 g) flour for a short pastry, and 1 tablespoon of water per 2 tablespoon (25 g) flour for suet or flaky pastries. Sometimes milk, cream, or yogurt is used instead of water to give a richer, shorter, more flavorsome pastry crust. Fruit juice can be used in sweet pastries to give more flavor—usually citrus juices are used with finely grated rind for increased zest.

Liquid is always added cold to a pastry with the exception of hot water crust, which is heated with the fat until melted and very hot. Where egg is added (see following notes), the liquid content is reduced.

4) Egg

Usually, only the yolk is added to pastry dough to enrich it in flavor, texture, and color. The extra liquid provided by adding the yolk to the mixture means that you will need to reduce the quantity of liquid you add in order to avoid an over-wet dough. Well-beaten whole egg is widely used in pastry making and, when brushed on raw pastry, is used as a glaze. Beaten egg white and a sprinkling of sugar gives a crisp coating to a sweet pie, whereas egg yolk on its own gives an ultrarich finish.

5) Salt

Adding this everyday condiment will help bring out the flavor of your savory and your sweet pastries. Make sure to measure salt correctly, especially when adding to a pastry being used for a sweet filling—follow the guidelines stated in the recipe. Season the filling carefully too, keeping in mind that your pastry already has a salt content.

6) Sugar

Sugar is added in small amounts to sweet pastries. White, fine, superfine (castor) or confectioner's (icing) sugars are most commonly used; these are most easily blended in a pastry dough, but soft light brown and dark sugars can be used for a more rustic pastry and will also give a more caramelized flavor and color to a baked pie crust—definitely worth experimenting with. Sweet pies are also often sprinkled with sugar to make a crust either before baking or just before serving. Demerara sugar gives an added crunchy finish to a pastry crust before baking.

7) Other Ingredients

To give a standard recipe a "twist," you can add small amounts of seasonings and flavorings to your mixture. Chopped fresh herbs, dried herbs, or spices can be used successfully in a savory pastry, and cinnamon, ginger, nutmeg, and ground mixed spice are great with fruit fillings, as are finely grated citrus zests. Cocoa powder can be substituted into a recipe instead of some of the flour content to make a chocolate-flavored pastry—add some sugar as well to reduce the bitterness. Liquid extracts or essences like vanilla, almond, or coffee can be used for flavor—add these before adding any other liquid to avoid making the pastry too wet. Ground nuts and small whole seeds can be used in addition to or instead of some of the flour for flavor and texture or for reasons of intolerance to wheat.

THE RULES FOR PASTRY MAKING

- The most important factor in pastry making is temperature. For all the pastries covered in this book, except hot water crust, you need to keep everything cool. Don't handle pastry more than you have to, and use only your fingertips to rub the fat into the flour—if you suffer from poor circulation like me, you'll have cold hands, which is a positive when it comes to pastry making! Rich short pastries and flaky pastries will benefit from resting in a cool place or in the fridge before rolling and shaping again to firm up the fat content.

- If you prefer a shortcut to rubbing in by hand, you can use a handheld mixer or food processor. It is always best to work the fat into the flour in short bursts, and the same is true of adding liquid; otherwise, there is a possibility that the pastry can become overmixed or processed and will be tough as a result. Refer to the manufacturer's instruction booklet for the correct settings and attachments.

- Add liquid in gradual, small amounts to avoid making the pastry dough too wet—if the mixture is too sticky, it will not only be difficult to handle but it will also dry out and harden too much on cooking. Avoid adding extra flour when rolling out if your pastry is too sticky; this will alter the proportion of ingredients and have a detrimental effect on the texture of the pastry by toughening the texture.

- Roll pastry in one direction. The easiest way is to roll it away from you—then, turn and roll it in the same "away from you" direction. For rounds of pastry, form the pastry into a ball first and then rotate as you roll, pinching together any cracks that appear on the edge. Being methodical with your turning and rolling technique means you are building a good, even structure to your pastry—particularly important for flaky pastry making when the rolling process helps form the flaky layers for the finished pastry. Use as little flour as possible to avoid drying out your pastry, and keep rolling to a minimum to avoid overhandling.

- Admittedly, some pastries are more difficult to handle (for example, those with a high fat content or low to no gluten). In this instance, it is better to try and loosen the pastry with a long, broad palette knife after every rolling and either slide the pastry around on the work top or, if this is too difficult, roll in a methodical fashion up and down and then side to side to achieve an even thickness.

- Most recipes in this book require you to roll out the pastry thinly. This means to a thickness of around ¼ inch (3–5 mm).

- Take care not to stretch the pastry to fit the tin or mold; the pastry will shrink back during cooking and may become misshapen.

- Most recipes call for freshly made or shaped pastry to rest or chill before filling or baking. Always cover the pastry in plastic wrap or, if it is in a block, wrap it in greaseproof paper. This will prevent a skin or crust from forming and will stop the pastry from drying out or picking up other flavors.

- Pastry is best cooked in a hot oven so that the fat doesn't "melt out" of the mixture but instead coats the flour particles quickly, enabling the dough to cook to a crisp. Everyone's oven heats up differently, so if you are concerned that your oven may not be heating up correctly, it is worth putting an oven thermometer on the center shelf of the oven in order to double-check the temperature.

- Short and flaky pastries can be stored for 2–5 days in the fridge if you don't want to use them immediately. You should wrap them well to avoid picking up flavors from other ingredients and to prevent a skin or crust from forming on the outside. Similarly, these pastries freeze well. Wrap tightly and freeze for up to 6 months and then allow them to defrost, still in the wrappings, in the fridge for a few hours until ready to use. Hot water crust pastry must be used while warm and fresh; otherwise, it will be too hard to handle. Allow a pastry to "warm up" slightly if it has been stored in the fridge—let it stand at room temperature for about 20 minutes before using.

A Word on Readymade Pastries

Some pastries are simply too time-consuming to make, and sometimes there just aren't enough hours in the day to make your own pastry, so for those occasions, we turn to readymade pastries. Shortcrust wheat flour pastry is available in fresh and frozen forms, for sweet and savory baking, in different flavors, and in block or ready rolled sheets. While this is my least favorite of the "readymades" (I'm not too fond of the flavor), it is a perfectly adequate compromise to making fresh. You do have to follow the guidelines on the packet, though, regarding using and resting times; otherwise, the pastry shrinks.

Readymade puff pastry is extremely popular and desirable with cooks and chefs alike; it really is a valuable substitute to the real thing. Available fresh, frozen, in blocks, or ready rolled; mixed fat and all-butter—I have had no failures or disappointments using these products. Again, read the guidelines given by the manufacturer for best results.

There are two other pastry types I use in this book which I have not attempted to make, and they are filo and brick. Both are extremely thin, wafer-like, leaf pastries which cook to a fine crisp. They are typically used in Mediterranean, North African, and Middle Eastern cookery. Filo pastry is now widely available in delicatessens, grocery stores, or supermarkets in fresh or frozen forms. It is usually wrapped in clear film and packaged in a long box. The size of the sheet varies, and I find the bigger sheets (around 15¾ x 12 inch/38 x 37 cm) easier to work with; if only smaller sheets are available, double up or overlap to create a bigger working area. Filo pastry dries out quickly, so keep unused sheets wrapped up or covered in damp kitchen paper. It is lower in fat than other pastries and is usually brushed with melted butter or oil before using in a pie in order to give a crisp finish; without the fat, filo is rather dry and leathery once cooked—beaten egg can be used to crisp up pastry, however, for a lower fat alternative. Filo pastry pies are best eaten hot or warm when the pastry is still crisp.

Brick pastry is a more specialist pastry but worth tracking down. It is used in North African pastries. It is also called "feuilles de brick," "brik," "briouat," and "oarka," depending on where and how it is used. It comes in wafer-thin rounds or squares of pastry which can be baked or fried. Unlike filo, it is not "greased" before using but still cooks to a delightful crisp. I have included a couple of recipes in my book which use this pastry to show you the techniques involved but also give instructions for using filo pastry as an alternative.

Pie Making Tips and Techniques

Once you've made your pastry or bought some, you need to know how to make your pie. There are several different ways you can present a pie, depending on how much pastry you want to use. As a huge pastry fan, I like my pies to have a bottom and a top, and I always feel a bit cheated if there's nothing at the bottom of the dish to hold my filling in place; but that's just personal preference and perhaps a touch of greediness too!

Individual recipes in the book give basic instructions for the pie stated, but below are some general pointers to help you achieve a good result.

1) PIE MAKING EQUIPMENT

The good news is that you don't really need anything special to make a pie.

- **Dishes, tins and molds:** Metallic or enamel pie dishes or tins come in various sizes and are reasonably priced; they are ideal for double crust pies; they conduct the heat well and help firm up the pastry base. Ceramic dishes are good for top crust pies; they should have a wide rim with which you can attach the pastry to the dish with ease. Pie plates have a wide rim and a gently dipping middle; they can be made of ceramic, enamel, or metal. Double crust pies are easier to cut when they are made in a pie plate, but you don't get much filling per portion. If there is lots of filling, choose a deep, earthenware pie dish; oval, square, or round in shape, and available in many sizes, these are the dishes for a pastry topped pie. For more specialist and fancy pies, you'll find metal pie molds and long loaf tins with hinged sides for easy release. Some molds have embossed and decorative sides that leave an impression on the pastry when it is cooked. Pies look pretty impressive baked in these tins, but these tins are more expensive to buy. Loose-bottomed and spring form tins are less expensive and less fancy but do enable you to produce a perfect free standing pie with a minimum of fuss.

- **Pie funnel (pie bird):** Pie funnels are usually made of ceramic or porcelain and shaped like a pointed chimney or a bird with its beak open. More contemporary funnels are available in bright colors made of silicone, and there are also novelty ones out there if you fancy starting a collection. Pie funnels let out steam from the pie filling as it bakes and help prevent the pastry top from becoming soggy by giving it a little support, keeping it slightly away from the filling. You can use a greased, large, metal piping nozzle if you don't have a specialist funnel or make your own by rolling up a double thickness of aluminum foil into a short, narrow tube.

- **Rolling pin and metal ruler:** Use a heavy, long rolling pin for best results. Wood is the most traditional, but marble is also good because it helps keep the pastry cool as well. Avoid any rolling pin with grooves or pits that will mark your pastry as you roll, and keep it clean to avoid transferring flavors. I have a 12-inch (30 cm) metal ruler that I find useful for kitchen use. It makes for a good cutting edge and also acts as a palette knife, helping release pastry from the work surface for easy turning.

- **Flour shaker or dredger:** This is useful but not essential. It does ensure you only get only a fine sifting of flour on your work surface when you are ready to roll out your pastry. Make sure the flour inside the shaker gets changed regularly—ideally, put only a small amount of flour in your shaker each time you use it. A sieve works just as well.

- **Baking beans:** Small, reusable, marble-like ceramic "beans" are used for weighing down an unfilled pastry case during baking. During baking, the pastry sets in position with the beans on top, and once the pastry sets, the beans can then be removed, and the empty pastry case can be put back in the oven to finish baking. You can use just as easily raw lentils or rice to achieve the same result.

- **Pastry board or mat:** Marble slabs are expensive and heavy but are perfect for keeping your pastry cool as you work. I have a cold, north-facing kitchen, so this is not something I ever need to consider, but I have certainly used marble in the past when conditions have been warmer. Pastry mats are reasonably priced and help you remove pastry after rolling, reducing the risk of tearing it.

- **Work surface:** Remember to make sure your work surface is thoroughly clean before you roll out your pastry—a spray of food-safe antibacterial spray and a good wipe down before you get started is all you need to do. If you have chips or marks in your work surface, keep in mind that these will get transferred onto your pastry if you roll out on such a surface.

Pie funnels or pie birds are usually made of ceramic or porcelain and shaped like a pointed chimney or a bird with its beak open.

2) Top Crust Pie

This type of pie is usually made in a deep pie dish. Put the filling in the dish so that it is very full and a little rounded on top—if you don't have quite enough filling, use a pie funnel to stop the pastry from sagging.

Roll out the pastry of choice to the required thickness, 2 inches (5 cm) wider than the pie dish. Wet the rim of the pie dish with water. Cut 1 inch (2.5 cm) wide strips of pastry from the outer edge of the rolled pastry and press them neatly onto the rim of the dish to cover the rim completely. Brush the pastry rim with water or beaten egg. Lift the remaining pastry onto the rolling pin and lay it over the pie dish. If you are using a pie funnel, you need to cut a cross in the center of the pastry first. Trim off the excess pastry with a sharp knife held at a slight angle away from the dish. Seal the pastry firmly by either pressing with your thumb and forefinger or using the prongs of a fork.

It is important to get a good seal on your pastry, and "knocking up" the edges is an extra insurance policy toward achieving this. Using a kitchen knife blade, make horizontal, shallow cuts in the side of the pastry edges to give the appearance of layers or pages in a book and merge the two layers together to seal. Do this all around the rim of pastry.

Pastry trimmings can be gathered, rolled, and used as a decoration on top of the pie lid. Cut a slit in the center of the pie crust for the steam to escape and glaze as directed. I prefer to bake all my pies in their dish on a baking tray, just in case any filling bubbles out during cooking. Some cooks like to preheat the baking tray in the oven as it warms up so that the pie goes straight onto a hot tray and gets cooking quicker; this is supposed to help cook a pastry bottom more crisply, but I'm not entirely sure it really makes that much difference.

3) Double Crusters

My favorite pie is one with a pastry top and bottom. Most are usually made with shortcrust, but you can use one of the flaky pastries, and sometimes you'll see a shortcrust pastry bottom with a flaky pastry lid. Divide the pastry in two, making one piece slightly bigger than the other. Roll the larger piece to the required thickness, to 1 inch (2.5 cm) bigger than the combined measurement of the diameter and sides of the dish—if you're using a shallow pie plate, then simply use the inverted pie plate as your guide. Lift the remaining pastry onto the rolling pin and lay it over the pie dish. If your chosen dish has sides, carefully fit the pastry into it, easing the pastry in place on the sides, taking care not to stretch or tear the pastry—if the pastry is short, you can patch the pastry together again by pinching and molding the pastry, sealing over any joins, and pressing them evenly to make a smooth case. Make sure there are no air pockets between the sides and the pastry. Trim the pastry as necessary.

Add your chosen cold filling, slightly rounding the surface; use a pie funnel if necessary. Brush the pastry rim with water or beaten egg. Roll out the remaining pastry to form the lid, making sure it is about ½ inch (1 cm) bigger than the pie dish, and lift the lid into position using your rolling pin. Cover the pie and seal the edge.

Trim as necessary and seal as described above. Decorate with trimmings if you like. Cut a slit in the center of the pie crust for the steam to escape and glaze as directed.

4) Bottom Crust Pie

Most bottom crust pies are usually made with a shortcrust pastry, which is usually baked without a filling ("baking blind"). However, I do include a few pies where the filling is baked in the pastry case and then given a topping which requires further baking. Loose-bottomed or spring form (spring tip) tins are useful for making pastry cases that you want to be free standing; for best results, lightly grease the tin and then baseline it with baking parchment. You can also use ceramic, shallow-sided pie or flan dishes for this type of pie and serve your pie straight from the dish. Again, if you line the bottom of the dish with baking parchment, you will be able to cut the pie and get it out of the dish more easily.

Roll out the pastry to the required thickness to the combined measurements of the diameter plus the sides of the tin or dish. Using a rolling pin, lift the pastry and lower it into the tin or dish. Carefully fit the pastry to the sides, easing it into place, taking care not to stretch or tear the pastry—if the pastry is short, you can patch the pastry together again by pinching and molding the pastry, sealing over any joins, pressing them evenly to make a smooth case. Make sure there are no air pockets between the sides and the pastry. Trim the pastry as necessary, leaving approximately ¼ inch (½cm) over the rim of the tin or dish.

To bake a pastry case "blind," cut a piece of baking parchment the same shape as your pastry case but slightly larger all around. Place it in the center of the pastry case and half-fill with ceramic baking beans or raw rice. Bake as directed in your recipe until set. Carefully remove the parchment and beans, prick the base with a fork, and return to the oven as directed to enable the base to dry out.

5) Individual Pies

For making smaller pies, the principles are the same as above, just scaled down. Take care not to stretch the pastry to fit the tins. Large pastry cutters or saucers make the perfect stencils for lining and covering round tins. For very small tins, simply break off a small knob of pastry, roll it into a ball, and press it into each tin; then, use your fingers to push and ease the pastry up the sides.

6) Raised Pie

Various pie recipes of different shapes and sizes using hot water crust pastry are given in the book along with full instructions for assembling them. The most important thing to remember when using this type of pastry is that it sets as it cools and becomes harder to work with. Keep the part of the pastry that is not being worked with covered under a cloth or an upside down bowl to reduce the cooling time.

Preparing the pastry
for "baking blind."

7) Pie Fillings

Because pastry has a high fat content, it melts easily and becomes greasy, and therefore, most pie fillings are cold when the pie is assembled. Pastry requires cooking at a relatively high temperature for a reasonably short time, so if your filling is raw, you need to ensure that it will cook thoroughly in the time it takes to cook the pastry. For this reason, many fillings are cooked and cooled in advance. Slow cooked meats such as stewing beef and mutton are casseroled first and then cooled before being used as a filling. Once they are cold, scrape off any fat that forms on the top to make the filling less greasy. These fillings benefit from a "second cooking" when reheated under a pie crust; they have more flavor and become meltingly tender.

Try to avoid adding too much gravy, sauce, or cooking liquor to a pie filling, especially if the pie has a pastry bottom; excess liquid will be absorbed by raw pastry and prevent it from becoming crisp, and it may also leak out over the sides of the dish, spoiling the appearance of the finished pie and resulting in insufficient filling retained under the pastry crust.

As with any food that requires reheating, make sure your filling cools as quickly as possible and is then covered and stored in the fridge until required for pie making. Always reheat pie fillings thoroughly—a digital food probe or thermometer inserted into the center of a cooked pie is an ideal way to dispel any doubts you may have about internal temperature.

If using a chilled filling, let the filling stand at room temperature for about 20 minutes before cooking so that it reheats quicker. Delicate textured pie fillings like fish, eggs, and soft fruit are only lightly cooked beforehand or used raw in order to preserve flavor and texture.

8) Pie Decorations and Finishing Techniques

You can transform the top of any pie from something very plain to something completely over the top by using up your pastry trimmings and making various shapes and decorations. There is a huge range of pastry cutters available these days in many sizes. Leaves used to be the most traditional shapes, but now you can find cutters to reflect just about any filling: I've got fish, birds, pigs, sheep, and cows for my pies, as well as a selection of fruit and vegetables, and even some bugs and beasts (perfect for children's parties!). Pastry stars are festive and seasonal, and hearts make any pie extra special; you can spell out the filling or personalize a pie with alphabet cutters or make up your own designs by cutting around a cardboard stencil or template. Simply stick pastry shapes onto the pie top using water or beaten egg and then glaze along with the rest of the pastry top. For a splash of color, leave the pastry decorations unglazed before baking and then, once baked, paint them with a light brushing of food coloring—this looks great on a cherry pie: simply paint small pastry rounds red and leaf shapes green.

TYPES OF PASTRY

SHORTCRUST PASTRY

Makes: 2 cups (450 g)   Preparation: 10 minutes plus chilling

Ingredients

1cup, 2 Tbsp. (250 g) flour
Pinch of salt
9 Tbsp. (125 g) half white
    fat (lard or vegetable
    equivalent) and half
    block margarine or
    unsalted butter, cut
    into small pieces
About 4 Tbsp. cold water

A widely used "short" pastry that is easily made, quick and simple to use, and forms the base, top, and sides of many savory and sweet dishes.

1. Mix the flour and salt together and add the pieces of fat.

2. Using both hands, rub the fat into the flour between finger and thumb tips. In a short while, you will see the mixture is well blended and resembles fresh breadcrumbs.

3. Sprinkle the water evenly over the pastry crumbs and stir with a round bladed knife until the mixture comes together in large lumps. Using one hand, scoop up the pieces and knead lightly for a few seconds to make a firm, smooth dough.

4. You can use this pastry right away, but it is better to leave it to stand or "rest" for 15 minutes in the bowl so that the flour can absorb the fat. For later use, wrap and chill for up to 2 days or freeze.

Variations

- Whole wheat and spelt (ancient wheat)—follow the basic recipe, but you may need to add a little more water to bring the mixture together. Blend half white flour with wholewheat flour to make a lighter crust.

- If you want to make a slightly richer pastry, increase the proportion of fat to 10 tablespoons (150 g)—you will need less water, approximately 3 tablespoons.

- For a simple sweet variation, add 3 tablespoons superfine (castor) sugar to the rubbed-in mixture.

- Fat reduced—it is possible to make shortcrust using less fat and more water—use 5 tablespoons (75 g) of fat, and you will need approximately 6 tablespoons water. The result will be a firmer, more chewy pastry, perfect for containing gravy- or sauce-rich fillings.

- Nut pastry—replace ¼ cup (50 g) of the flour with ground or finely chopped unsalted nuts such as walnuts, hazelnuts, almonds, or pecans. Can be used with savory and sweet dishes and has a softer texture than an all-wheat shortcrust.

WHEAT-FREE AND GLUTEN-FREE SHORTCRUST

Makes: 2 cups (450 g)   Preparation: 10 minutes

Ingredients

9 Tbsp. (125 g) brown
  rice flour
9 Tbsp. (125 g) soya flour
½ tsp. gluten free baking
  powder
9 Tbsp. (125 g) unsalted
  butter or margarine
4 Tbsp. cold water

There are so many varieties of gluten free flour available. Without gluten, pastry is much softer and more crumbly in texture than traditional shortcrust; it needs to be handled a bit differently. If only wheat gluten is a problem, you can make a very tasty pastry using finely ground oats.

1. Mix the flours and baking powder together. Cut the fat into small pieces and toss into the flour.

2. Using both hands, rub the fat into the flour between finger and thumb tips. In a short while, you will see the mixture is well blended and resembles fresh breadcrumbs.

3. Sprinkle the water evenly over the pastry crumbs and stir with a round bladed knife until the mixture begins to come together in large lumps. Using one hand, scoop up the pieces and knead lightly for a few seconds to make a soft dough.

4. This pastry is ready to use right away, but it is much softer than other pastries, and you may find it only suitable for lining a tin at this stage. For later use, wrap and chill for up to 2 days or freeze. Chilling will firm up the pastry dough and give you more options for using it as per your chosen recipe.

Variations

- For an oat pastry, replace the 2 flours above with 1 cup 2 tablespoons (250 g) porridge oats which you blitz in a blender or food processor to make a fine powder.

- For a sweet version, add 2–3 teaspoons of superfine (castor) or light brown sugar to the blended pastry crumbs.

- Replace soya flour with chickpea (gram) flour for a really nutty, savory pastry; buckwheat flour will also give a nutty, earthy flavor. Both flours are best suited to savory dishes. You will need to add more water with different gluten free flours because the absorption rate varies between different types.

- You can also use finely ground nuts as one of the flours in the recipe—ground almond or chestnuts make a deliciously rich, crumbly pastry for a sweet dish.

SUET CRUST

Ingredients

14 Tbsp. (200 g)
     self-rising flour
¾ tsp salt
7 Tbsp. (100 g) shredded
     beef or vegetable suet
½ cup (150 ml) cold water

This is a pastry from yesteryear. It went out of fashion for several years due to increased health awareness, but now there is a vegetable alternative to traditional beef suet. This means that suet crust, the easiest-of-all pastries to make, is back on the menu.

1. Mix together the flour, salt, and suet. Add enough cold water, mixing at the same time, to make a light, elastic dough.

2. Turn onto a lightly floured surface and knead very gently until smooth.

3. This pastry should be used right away because the rising agent will begin activating once the flour is mixed with water. Suet crust pastry can be used for sweet and savory dishes and can be steamed as well as baked.

Variations

- Use the same quantity all purpose (plain) flour if you prefer and add 2½ teaspoons of baking powder.

- Use whole wheat self-rising flour or spelt flour plus baking powder for a more wholesome pastry, but you will probably need to add a bit more water.

- Add chopped herbs or spices to the mixture for flavored doughs. Finely grated citrus rind gives a nice tangy twist for a sweet pastry crust.

OIL PASTRY

Ingredients

1½ cups (350 g) flour
½ tsp salt
½ cup (115 ml) sunflower
    or vegetable oil
4 Tbsp. cold water

A type of shortcrust pastry made using a vegetable oil instead of hard fat. It is more difficult to work with than standard, hard, fat-based shortcrust but offers different flavor options. Take into account that the oil you choose will affect the color and flavor of your finished dish. Use nut oils sparingly because they overheat during intensive cooking—they are best blended with a more heat tolerant, neutral-tasting oil such as sunflower.

Note: This is a slightly more greasy pastry than one made with solid fat, and it lends itself better to savory recipes rather than sweet. You may find it difficult to roll because it is inclined to stick to the rolling pin; therefore, you may find it easier to patch pieces together when lining a tin. A good solution to patching a top crust together is to cut out shapes of pastry using a cutter and overlap them on top of the pie filling to form a layer.

1. Mix together the flour and salt in a bowl. Make a well in the center and add the oil. Mix until well-blended.

2. Gradually blend in the water until the mixture comes together to form a firm dough.

3. Turn onto a lightly floured surface and knead very gently until smooth. Rest for 10 minutes before using.

Variations

- Heat-tolerant, cold-pressed rapeseed oil and standard olive oil will add more flavor to your pastry.

- If you want to enhance the nutty flavor in a dish, replace 2 teaspoons of a standard vegetable oil with walnut, hazelnut, or sesame seed oil. Nut and seed oils are not heat-tolerant, so use no more than this quantity; otherwise, the flavor will be lost or affected.

- Replace white flour with whole wheat or spelt for a more wholesome pastry.

- It is difficult to make a decent gluten-free pastry using oil because it becomes very greasy, but some success can be had by blending buckwheat flour with brown rice flour and using sunflower oil.

SOFT CHEESE PASTRY

Makes: 2 cups, 3 Tbsp. (500 g)   Preparation: 10 minutes plus chilling

Ingredients

10 Tbsp. (150 g) unsalted
    butter, softened
10 Tbsp. (150 g) full fat
    soft cheese
14 Tbsp. (20 g) flour
pinch of salt

There are several ways you can make cheese pastry, depending on how cheesy you want the flavor of your pastry to be; recipes are usually based on shortcrust. Below are 2 variations ranging from the mild to the more flavored.

Note: This is a very short pastry which can be difficult to work, so chilling is essential. It has a delicious melt-in-the-mouth texture and slight flakiness that will make it worth the effort. It requires a short cooking time at a high temperature, so is only suitable for fillings that require little cooking or heating through.

1. In a mixing bowl, beat together the butter and soft cheese until well blended. Sift the flour and salt on top. Stir until evenly mixed and then use your hands to bring the mixture together to form a firmish dough.

2. Turn onto a floured surface and knead gently until smooth—you may need to use more flour with this pastry because it is quite sticky. Wrap and chill for 2 hours before using.

Variations:

• Add chopped herbs for extra flavor in a savory pie.

• Replace white flour with whole wheat or spelt flour for a more wholesome flavor.

DOUBLE CHEESE PASTRY

Makes: 1¾ cup, 1 Tbsp. (425 g)   Preparation: 10 minutes plus chilling

Very cheesy, this pastry will add extra savor to meat, chicken, fish, and vegetarian pies.

1. In a mixing bowl, beat together the butter with the soft cheese and egg yolk. Sift the flour on top and add the grated cheese and salt. Stir until evenly mixed and then use your hands to bring the mixture together to form a firm dough.

2. Turn onto a lightly floured surface and knead lightly until smooth; then, wrap and chill for 1 hour before using.

Variations:

- Add chopped chives to either recipe for a cheese and onion pastry.

- A pinch of dry mustard added to the flour helps bring out the cheese flavor, and 1 teaspoon smoked paprika adds a touch of color and smokiness to a cheesy pastry. Ground cumin or whole cumin seeds give an extra spicy twist to this pastry.

Ingredients

5 Tbsp. (75 g) unsalted butter, softened
5 Tbsp. (75 g) full fat soft cheese
1 egg yolk
¾ cup (175 g) flour
5 Tbsp. (75 g) freshly grated Parmesan cheese
½ tsp salt

PÂTE SUCRÉE (SUGAR PASTRY)

Makes: 2 cups (450g)   Preparation: 20 minutes plus chilling

Ingredients

14 Tbsp. (200 g) flour
¼ tsp. salt
3 medium egg yolks
7 Tbsp. (100 g) unsalted
    butter
7 Tbsp. (100 g) superfine
    (castor) sugar

A French enriched shortcrust pastry which can be rolled thin and holds its shape well. It has a crisp texture that melts in the mouth with butteriness. Pâte sucrée is the pastry traditionally used for continental pâtisserie. It is best made with white flour.

1. Sift the flour and salt directly onto the work surface in a pyramid shape.

2. Make an indent in the top and add the egg yolks. Cut the butter into small pieces and place on top. Sprinkle the sugar over the rest of the mixture.

3. Using a palette knife, cover the top with flour from each side of the pile. Using the fingertips of one hand, pinch the dry and wet ingredients together until all the flour is incorporated and the ingredients are well blended, making sure you keep bringing all the ingredients back into a pile as you work them together.

4. Work the dough quickly and lightly to make a smooth dough and form it into a ball. Wrap and chill for at least 1 hour before using.

Variations:

- Some recipes include ½–1 teaspoons (2.5–5ml) good quality vanilla for added flavor; you may prefer to add this extract or try good quality almond extract.

- If you want to add further flavors to your pastry, try adding finely grated, unwaxed citrus zest or ground spices such as ginger, nutmeg, cinnamon, or mixed spice.

HOT WATER CRUST PASTRY

Makes: 3½ cups (800 g)   Preparation: 10 minutes plus resting

This is a classic free standing pie pastry associated with lots of pies, from the everyday picnic pork or fruit pies to the gloriously elaborate raised game pies of celebration banquets. It is mixed with boiling water which makes it pliable to mold, and as it cools, it sets in shape and becomes firm. It is best made with white flour.

1. Mix the flour and salt together in a heatproof mixing bowl and make a well in the centre.

2. Put the fat in a saucepan with the water. Heat gently until melted and then bring to a boil.

3. Remove from the heat and quickly pour into the well all in one motion. Working quickly, mix the ingredients together using a wooden spoon until well blended.

4. When the mixture is just cool enough to touch, use one hand to bring the dough together and knead until smooth and silky. Cover loosely with a clean tea towel and leave to rest for 5 minutes before using.

Variations:
• Using bread (strong plain) flour gives a more substantial crust to a pie, which is perfect for large or hand-raised pies. Hot water crust made with all purpose (plain) flour has a more pliable texture and is good for making smaller pies in tins and for use with sweet fillings.

Ingredients

2 cups (450 g) flour
1½ tsp salt
7 Tbsp. (100 g) lard
   or solid white
   vegetable fat
1 cup, 2 Tbsp.
   (250 ml) water

FLAKY PASTRY

Makes: 2 cups (450 g)   Preparation: 30 minutes plus chilling

Ingredients

14 Tbsp. (200 g) bread
    (strong plain) or all
    purpose (plain) flour
pinch of salt
10 Tbsp. (150 g) half
    unsalted butter and
    half lard or solid white
    vegetable fat
1 Tbsp. fresh lemon juice
7 Tbsp. (100 ml)
    cold water

This is the most common of all the flaked pastries and can be used in sweet and savory cooking. Don't be daunted by the instructions; the method isn't as complicated as it looks. It is best with white flour.

1. Mix together the flour and salt. Put the fat on a plate. Using a small palette knife or round bladed kitchen knife, carefully press to gently soften the fat and then divide into 4 equal amounts.

2. Using both hands, rub one quarter of the fat into the flour between finger and thumb tips until well blended.

3. Add the lemon juice and sufficient water, stirring with a round bladed knife until the mixture comes together to make a firm, elastic dough.

4. Lightly flour the work surface and roll out the dough into a rectangle 4 x 12 inch (10 x 30 cm). Arrange another quarter of the fat, in small pieces, evenly over the top two-thirds of the dough.

5. Fold the bottom third of the dough up over the middle section (see picture right), and then fold down the top third of the dough on top with the fat inside. Turn the dough around 90° so that the folds are now at the side and gently press the edges together to seal using your rolling pin.

6. Reroll the dough into the long rectangle as before and continue the process using another portion of the fat, folding and turning as before. Repeat to use up the last portion of fat and then roll and fold the dough twice more to thoroughly incorporate the fat.

7. Wrap the pastry loosely in baking parchment and chill for at least 30 minutes. After this time, the pastry will be ready to use immediately or wrap well and store in the fridge for up to 3 days.

ROUGH PUFF PASTRY

Ingredients

3½ Tbsp. (200 g) bread
    (strong plain) or all
    purpose (plain) flour
pinch of salt
2½ Tbsp. (150 g) unsalted
    butter and lard or solid
    white vegetable fat
1 Tbsp fresh lemon juice
1¾ Tbsp. (100 ml)
    cold water

Similar to flaky but simpler to prepare. It does give a slightly more higgledy-piggledy result when baked, but can be used in all recipes where flaky is required, although where an even rise is called for (vol au vents) it is advisable to use flaky. Choose the rough puff method if you find flaky too much of a chore or have less time available.

1. Mix together the flour and salt. Cut the fat into small pieces about ¾ inch (2 cm) thick and toss into the flour without breaking them up.

2. Add the lemon juice and sufficient water, stirring with a round bladed knife until the mixture comes together to make a fairly stiff dough.

3. Lightly flour the work surface and roll out the dough into a rectangle 4 x 12 inch (10 x 30 cm).

4. Fold the bottom third of the dough up over the middle section, and then fold down the top third of the dough on top. Turn the dough around 90° so that the folds are now at the side and gently press the edges together to seal using your rolling pin (see picture opposite).

5. Reroll the dough into the long rectangle as before, and continue the process folding and turning as before. Repeat the rolling and folding 3 more times (5 times in total) until the fat is incorporated.

6. Wrap the pastry loosely in baking parchment and chill for at least 30 minutes before using. This will make the pastry easier to handle. After this time, the pastry will be ready to use immediately or wrap well and store in the fridge for up to 3 days.

PUFF PASTRY

Serves: 2 cups, 5 Tbsp. (525 g)   Preparation: 40 minutes plus chilling

Ingredients

14 Tbsp. (200 g) strong
   plain or all purpose
   (plain) flour
pinch of salt
14 Tbsp. (200 g) pieces
   unsalted butter
1 Tbsp. fresh lemon juice
7 Tbsp. (100 ml)
   cold water

The richest of all pastries; most even rising, most buttery, flakiest, and the crispiest of flaky pastries—but time consuming to make, so you may want to save this one for a special occasion. Puff pastry making requires careful preparation and is best made the day before you want to use it. Puff pastry can be used for sweet or savory dishes. Readymade puff pastry is widely available fresh and frozen and is probably the most successful of all commercially produced pastries. Puff pastry is best made with white flour and unsalted butter.

Note: if your pastry has been stored in the fridge for a while, allow it to stand at room temperature for about 20 minutes before baking.

1. Mix together the flour and salt. Using your fingertips, rub 2 tablespoons (25 g) butter into the flour until well blended.

2. Put the remaining butter on a board. Using a small palette knife or round bladed kitchen knife, carefully press the butter to gently soften it, keeping it in one piece, and then form into a rectangle about 4 inches (10 cm) long.

3. Add the lemon juice and sufficient water to the flour, stirring with a round bladed knife until the mixture comes together to make a fairly stiff dough.

4. Lightly flour the work surface and roll out the dough to make a 9-inch (23 cm) square. Place the piece of butter on one half. Fold over the dough to enclose the butter and seal the edges using your rolling pin.

5. Turn the dough so that the fold is at the side and then roll into a rectangle approximately 34 inches (40 cm) long.

6. Fold the bottom third of the dough up over the middle section and then fold down the top third of the dough on top and gently press the edges together to seal using your rolling pin. Roll into a rectangle again and repeat the folding and sealing. Wrap the pastry loosely in baking parchment and chill for 30 minutes to rest.

7. Put the pastry back down on a lightly floured surface so that the fold is on the side and continue to roll, fold, seal, and rest 4 more times as in step 6. After this time, the pastry will be ready to use immediately or wrap well and store in the fridge for up to 3 days.

MEAT

STEW AND DUMPLING PIE

Serves: 4–6   Preparation: 30 minutes plus cooling   Cooking: 3 hours 50 minutess

Ingredients

3 cups (675 g) stewing beef
    such as shin, brisket,
    blade, or chuck steak,
    cut into ¾ inch
    (2 cm) thick pieces
3 Tbsp flour
salt and freshly ground
    black pepper
2 Tbsp. (25 g) dripping or
    butter
1 Tbsp. vegetable oil
1 large onion, peeled and
    chopped
4 pieces rindless unsmoked
    streaky bacon, chopped
2 cups (450 g) carrots,
    peeled and sliced
1½ cups (450 ml) beef stock
2 bay leaves
1 quantity suet crust pastry
    with 2 Tbsp. chopped
    parsley and 3 Tbsp.
    creamed horseradish
    sauce added
1 egg, beaten, to glaze

For a proper, really tasty meat pie, you need to make up the filling in advance, which requires a bit of forethought and planning. Here, a traditional beef stew is made and then the next day used as the base for a hearty suet crust topped pie. It makes a great meal served simply with green vegetables.

1. Put the beef in a bowl. Toss in the flour and season well. Mix together, making sure the beef is well coated in the flour.

2. Melt the dripping or butter in a large saucepan until bubbling and fry the beef with the flour, stirring, for about 5 minutes until browned all over. Using a draining spoon, transfer the beef to a heatproof plate.

3. Reheat the pan juices with the oil and gently fry the onion and bacon for 5 minutes until softened; then, mix the beef back into the pan along with the carrots, stock, and bay leaves.

4. Bring to a boil, stirring occasionally, and then cover and simmer very gently for about 2½ hours, or until very tender. Allow to cool and discard the bay leaves. Transfer to a 5½ cup (1.65 L) oval pie dish with rim 10 x 7x3 inch (25 x 18 x 7.5 cm). Push a pie funnel in the centrer. Cover and chill until required.

5. To make the pie, preheat the oven to 425°F (220°C). Roll out the pastry on a lightly floured surface to just larger than the pie dish. Make a cross in the center for the pie funnel. Carefully cut some of the excess pastry into thin strips and secure on to the edge of the pie dish with water. Brush with egg. Transfer the rolled out pastry to the top and press down on to the edge using a fork. Brush all over with egg.

6. Put the dish on a baking tray and bake for 10 minutes; then, reduce the temperature to 375°F (190°C, 170°C fan oven) and cook for a further 50 minutes to 1 hour until crisp and golden and the meat is piping hot—cover with foil if the pastry browns too quickly. Serve immediately.

STEAK AND KIDNEY DOUBLE CRUST

Serves: 4   Preparation: 30 minutes plus cooling   Cooking: 3 hour 15 minutes

---

There are several ways you can make up this classic pie, but I always go back to a top and bottom pastry pie for complete deliciousness. Leave out the kidney if you prefer. As with many pies, you need to start this one a few hours before to make sure the filling is completely cold before you assemble your pie.

1. Put the beef and kidney in a bowl. Toss in the flour and season well. Mix together, making sure the meat is well coated in the flour.

2. Melt the fat in a large saucepan until bubbling and fry the beef and kidney with the flour and onion, stirring, for about 5 minutes until browned all over.

3. Add a few slugs of Worcestershire sauce and sufficient cold water to barely cover the meat. Bring to a boil, stirring occasionally, then cover and simmer very gently for about 2½ hours, or until very tender. Allow to cool then cover and chill until required. Remove any fat that sets on the surface.

4. To make the pie, preheat the oven to 400°F (200°C, 180°C fan oven). Roll out the shortcrust pastry on a lightly floured work surface to cover the base of a 9½ x 1¾ inch (24 x 4 cm) round pie dish with rim. Trim as necessary and spoon the cold meat filling into the pastry case. Brush the edge of the pastry with beaten egg.

5. Roll out the flaky pastry to cover the pie dish. Trim to neaten and pinch the edges of the pastry together to seal. Make a hole in the centre and brush all over with beaten egg. Stand the pie dish on a baking tray and bake in the oven for about 40 minutes until richly golden and the filling is piping hot. Best served hot with extra Worcestershire sauce.

Ingredients

2 cups (450 g) stewing beef such as shin, brisket, blade or chuck steak, cut into ¾ inch (2 cm) thick pieces
1 cup (225 g) ox, pig's or sheep's kidneys, skinned, cored and chopped
3 Tbsp. flour
salt and freshly ground black pepper
2 Tbsp. (25 g) dripping, lard, or vegetable fat
1 onion, peeled and sliced
Worcestershire sauce to taste
½ quantity shortcrust pastry
½ quantity flaky pastry
1 egg, beaten, to glaze

PUB GRUB (BEEF AND ALE)

Makes: 4   Preparation: 30 minutes plus cooling   Cooking: 3 hours 20 minutes

Ingredients

3 cups (675 g) stewing
beef such as shin,
brisket, blade, or chuck
steak, cut into ¾ inch
(2 cm) thick pieces
3 Tbsp. flour
Salt and freshly ground
black pepper
2 Tbsp. (25 g) dripping
or butter
1 Tbsp. vegetable oil
1 onion, peeled and
chopped
4 field or flat mushrooms,
peeled and sliced
8 pieces of rindless
smoked streaky bacon,
chopped
1½ cups (450 ml) bitter ale
or similar
A small bunch fresh
thyme, tied with
clean string
½ quantity flaky pastry
1 egg, beaten, to glaze

Any self-respecting pub will have a pie on their menu, and those specializing in different types of local brews and beers often reflect the fact in their cooking too. The final choice is up to you, but I like "Newcastle Brown" in my pie (plus a little bit more to wash it down!). Cheers!

1. Put the beef in a bowl. Toss in the flour and season well. Mix together, making sure the beef is well coated in the flour.

2. Melt the dripping or butter in a large saucepan until bubbling and fry the beef with the flour, stirring, for about 5 minutes until browned all over. Using a draining spoon, transfer the beef to a heatproof plate.

3. Reheat the pan juices with the oil and gently fry the onion, mushrooms and bacon for 5 minutes until softened; then, put the beef back into the pan along with the bitter ale and thyme.

4. Bring to a boil, stirring occasionally, and then cover and simmer very gently for about 2½ hours or until very tender. Allow to cool, discard the thyme, and then transfer to 1 cup (4 x 300 ml) individual pie dishes. Cover and chill until required.

5. To make up the pies, preheat the oven to 425°F (220°C, 200°C fan oven). Divide the pastry into 4 equal pieces and roll out each piece on a lightly floured surface to just larger than the tops of the pie dishes. Carefully cut some of the excess pastry into thin strips and secure onto the edge of the pie dishes with water. Brush with egg. Transfer the rolled out pastry to the tops, trim, and press down onto the edge using a fork..

6. If you prefer, roll out any leftover trimmings and use pastry cutters to make your chosen design. Stick on top of the pie using beaten egg. Make a hole in the center and brush the pastry all over with egg.

7. Put the dishes on a large baking tray and bake for 15 minutes and then reduce the temperature to 375°F (190°C, 170°C fan oven) and cook for a further 25 minutes until risen and golden and the meat is piping hot. Serve immediately.

Variation

If you like a dark, rich flavor, choose a stout or Guinness; old fashioned "best bitter" will give you a hoppy, yeasty gravy, while light ales and lagers make a mellower liquor. Use half water and half beer for a less yeasty flavor.

MUFFIN TIN CORNED BEEF AND BEAN PIES

Makes: 9   Preparation: 25 minutes   Cooking: 40 minutes

Some pies are best served straight from the oven, but these are fine served cold, ideal for a picnic or packed lunch with tomato ketchup or chutney. No advance filling preparation required either (you can even use up leftovers), so if you fancy a pie in a hurry, here's one to try.

1. Roll out the pastry thinly on a lightly floured surface, and stamp out 4 inch (9 x 10 cm) rounds using a pastry cutter, rerolling the pastry as necessary.

2. Carefully press each pastry circle into 2¾ inch (7 cm) diameter, 1¼ inch (3½ cm) deep muffin tins. Chill while you make the topping.

3. Preheat the oven to 400°F (200°C, 180°C fan oven). Put the butter or margarine in a bowl and beat in the flour until it is well blended and forms a rich, crumbly mixture. Stir in the grated cheese.

4. Divide the potato between each pastry case. Mash the corned beef with the tomato ketchup and pile on top of the potato; then add a layer of baked beans. Pile the cheesy crumble on top to cover the filling. Bake in the oven for about 40 minutes until golden and piping hot. Cool in the tins for 10 minutes before serving or transfer to a wire rack to cool completely; then, wrap and chill until ready to serve.

Variation

If corned beef's not your thing, you can use any cooked leftover minced or finely chopped meat or chicken in this recipe.

Ingredients

1 quantity whole wheat or spelt shortcrust pastry
4 Tbsp. (50 g) butter or margarine, softened
9 Tbsp. (125 g) whole wheat or spelt flour
5 Tbsp. (75 g) mature Cheddar cheese, grated
1 cup (225 g) cold mashed potato
½ cup (115 g) corned beef
2 Tbsp. tomato ketchup
¾ cup (175 g) canned baked beans in tomato sauce

SCOTTISH (COO) PIES

Makes: 9   Preparation: 45 minutes   Cooking: 40 minutes

When I moved to Scotland a few years ago, I found myself in "pie heaven." All the local bakeries sell umpteen pastry creations, and meat pies are probably the most popular and famous. This is my version of a classic Scotch beef handheld pie.

1. Put the ground beef in a bowl and mix in the fat, onion, turnip or rutabaga (swede), salt, and plenty of pepper. Divide into 9 portions and form each into a burger shape approximately 3¼ inch (8 cm) diameter. Set aside.

2. Make up the hot water crust pastry. Keep the remainder of the pastry warm while preparing each of the pies. Set aside one quarter of the pastry and keep covered.

3. Roll out the remaining pastry thinly on a lightly floured work surface, and using a 6-inch (15 cm) pastry cutter or upturned saucer, stamp out 9 circles, rerolling the pastry as necessary.

4. Taking one piece of pastry at a time, place a portion of meat in the center. Bring up the sides of the pastry to enclose the meat, leaving the top open, and bring the pastry up about ½ inch (1 cm) higher than the filling. Flatten the bottom and smooth the sides to neaten the shape. Place on a lightly greased baking tray. Repeat to use up the remaining pastry circles and filling.

5. Preheat the oven to 400°F (200°C, 180°C fan oven). Roll out the remaining pastry thinly and cut out 3 ¼-inch (9 x 8 cm) circles, rerolling as necessary. Brush the inside of each pie with beaten egg and push a pastry circle on top of the meat. Pinch the pastry edges together to seal.

Ingredients

- 2¼ cups (500 g) lean Aberdeen Angus beef steak mince (ground beef)
- 2 Tbsp. (25 g) beef suet or melted butter
- 1 onion, peeled and finely chopped
- 10 Tbsp. (150 g) turnip or rutabaga (swede), peeled and grated
- 1 tsp salt
- Freshly ground pepper
- 1 quantity hot water crust pastry
- 1 egg, beaten, to glaze

6. If you prefer, roll out any pastry trimmings quite thickly and cut out 9 pairs of cow horn-shaped pieces. Place on another lightly greased baking tray.

7. In the top of each pie, make a central slit for steam to escape if you are making undecorated pies; otherwise, cut 2 slits either side where the pastry horns can be inserted. Brush the pie tops with egg and also the pastry horns if made.

8. Bake the pies for 40 minutes until richly golden and the filling is piping hot. The pastry horns will take about 15 minutes. Serve the pies hot or cold and insert a pair of pastry horns in the top if you like. Good with tomato ketchup!

EASTENDERS

Makes: 4   Preparation: 30 minutes   Cooking: 40 minutes

At the start of my career, I worked on a well-known woman's magazine. Our kitchen helper was a lovely lady from East London. One day, she brought us in traditional "pie and mash" for lunch. To be honest, it wasn't my ideal lunch, but for supper, it would have been just perfect. Here's my interpretation, many years later.

1. Preheat the oven to 375°F (190°C, 170°C fan oven). Put the minced beef in a bowl and add water; then, mix in the flour, onion, nutmeg, and plenty of seasoning.

2. Set aside one third of the pastry and divide the remainder into 4 equal pieces. Roll each piece of pastry thinly on a lightly floured surface to fit 4 nonstick 4½ tablepoon (250 ml) pie dishes with rims 5¼ x 6 x 1¼ inch (13½ x 10 x 3 cm) and line each one, covering the rim as well. Trim as necessary.

3. Divide the filling between each tin, pressing it into the case. Roll out the remaining pastry thinly to make lids to fit inside the pie tin, directly on top of the meat. Lay the lids on top of the meat and press down to fit snugly.

4. Brush the inside of the pastry with egg; then, fold over the pastry from the rim, pressing with your thumb at intervals to make a "crimped" edge inside the tin. Make a slash in the center of each, place on a baking tray, and brush with milk. Bake in the oven for about 40 minutes until golden and the filling is piping hot.

5. Meanwhile, make the "liquor." Put the cornstarch in a saucepan and gradually blend in half the milk to make a paste. Stir in the remaining milk along with the stock. Heat, stirring, until boiling, and cook for 1 minute until thickened. Remove from the heat and stir in the parsley, coloring if using, and season to taste. Set aside until ready to serve.

Ingredients

1½ cups (35 g) lean
    ground (minced) beef
4 Tbsp. cold water
2 Tbsp. (25 g) flour
1 small onion, peeled and
    grated
pinch of ground nutmeg
salt and freshly ground
    black pepper
1 quantity fat reduced
    shortcrust pastry
2 Tbsp. whole milk, to
    glaze

For the "liquor:"
2 Tbsp. cornstarch
    (cornflour)
½ cup (150 ml) whole milk
1 cup (300 ml) chicken or
    vegetable stock
6 Tbsp. freshly chopped
    parsley
green food coloring,
    optional

6. Just before serving, reheat the sauce for 2–3 mins. Turn the hot pies out of the tins, break the pastry tops and pour the liquor over them. Accompany with mashed potato and mushy peas.

Variation

Standard shortcrust pastry works just as well for this recipe but gives a shorter crust.

BEEF AND ONION CLANGER

Serves: 4–6   Preparation: 25 minutes plus cooling   Cooking: 55 minutes

I remember making a version of this dish in my school home economics class. The dish originates from Bedfordshire in England when it was served up to the workers with meat at one end and fruit at the other—rather like the original Cornish pasties. This all-savory roly-poly pie uses the traditional suet crust pastry associated with the original recipe.

1. First, make the filling. Put the ground beef in a saucepan with the onion and curry powder. Fry gently, stirring, for about 5 minutes to brown all over.

2. Remove from the heat, season well, and stir in the flour and gradually mix in the stock. Return to heat, and slowly bring to a boil, stirring until thickened. Reduce the heat, and simmer gently for 5 minutes. Set aside to cool completely and then stir in the frozen peas and sultanas.

3. To assemble the clanger, preheat the oven to 375°F (190°C, 170°C fan oven). Lightly grease a large baking tray. Make up the suet crust pastry and roll out on a lightly floured surface to make a 12 x 10-inch (30 x 25 cm) rectangle.

4. Spread with the cold ground beef mixture, leaving a border of about ¾ inch (2 cm) at the ends of the shorter sides. Brush the ends with beaten egg and carefully roll up from one of the shorter sides. Press lightly to seal the edge and place seam-side down on the baking tray. Brush all over with beaten egg and bake for about 45 minutes until golden brown and piping hot. Best served hot or warm.

Ingredients

¾ cup (175 g) lean ground (minced) beef
1 small onion, peeled and finely chopped
2 tsp. mild curry powder
salt and freshly ground black pepper
1 Tbsp. flour
½ cup (150 ml) beef stock
5 Tbsp. (75 g) frozen peas
2 Tbsp. (25 g) sultanas
1 quantity suet crust pastry, made up with 4 Tbsp. freshly chopped cilantro (coriander)
1 egg, beaten, to glaze

Variation

Follow the basic rolling and baking principles for making a baked jam roly-poly pudding—you will need 6–8 tablespoons of softened strawberry or jam to fill the pudding—I prefer to use vegetable suet for sweet dishes. Serve hot with custard.

MINI PASTY BITES

Makes: 18   Preparation: 45 minutes   Cooking: 40 minutes

Ingredients

¾ cup (175 g) peeled
   potato
½ cup (115 g) peeled
   turnip or rutabaga
   (swede)
1 small onion, peeled and
   finely chopped
1 cup (225 g) chuck steak,
   trimmed and finely
   diced
salt and freshly ground
   black pepper
1 quantity shortcrust
   pastry
2 Tbsp. (25 g) butter
1 egg, beaten, to glaze

We spent many family holidays in the southwest of England when I was growing up with freshly baked homemade pasties on the beach for a picnic. The Cornish pasty is a truly sacred pastry, and I won't attempt to replicate it. Instead I'm basing mine on happy memories.

1. Preheat the oven to 400°F (200°C, 180°C fan oven). Lightly grease a large baking tray. Cut the potatoes and rutabaga (swede) into thin slices and then cut the slices into short strips. Place in a bowl and mix in the onion, steak, and plenty of seasoning.

2. Roll out the pastry thinly on a lightly floured surface. Using a round pastry cutter, stamp out 4-inch (18 x 10 cm) rounds, rerolling the pastry as necessary.

3. Divide the filling and put some in the center of each and dot with a little butter. Brush the edges of the pastry with egg and fold each over to make a half moon shape. Press the edges together to seal.

4. Stand each pasty on its folded end, seam-side up, and carefully crimp the edges together between your thumb and forefinger—alternatively, keep the pasties on their side and press the edges with a fork.

5. Place on the baking tray and brush all over with egg to glaze and bake for 10 minutes. Reduce the temperature to 350°F (180°C, 160°C fan oven) and continue to cook for a further 30 minutes until golden and cooked through. Delicious served hot or cold.

Variation

For larger pasties, use a 6 inch (15 cm) cutter or saucer to make pastry rounds. Fill and fold in the same way. Bake as above, but extend the cooking time by 10–15 minutes at the lower temperature.

DINGLES

A great name for a pie. Originating from the Dingle region in County Kerry, Ireland, these mutton or lamb pies were sold on market days and made a filling, portable lunch for the shepherds of the area. To be traditional, use shortcrust pastry, but I like mine with a flaky pastry.

1. First, make the filling. Heat the oil in a saucepan and gently fry the onion, carrot, and lamb with the thyme and plenty of seasoning for 5 minutes, stirring, until the lamb is browned all over.

2. Stir in the flour and gradually stir in the stock. Bring to a boil; then, simmer gently, half covered, for 1 hour or until tender. Set aside to cool.

3. For the pies, preheat the oven to 425°F (220°C, 200°C fan oven). Line a large baking tray with baking parchment. Divide the pastry into 2 equal pieces and roll out each on a lightly floured surface to make a 12-inch (30 cm)square. Using a 6-inch (15 cm) round cutter or upside down saucer, stamp out 4 circles from each. Discard the trimmings.

4. Divide the filling between 4 circles. Brush the edges with water and place another circle on top. Seal the edges together by pressing with the prongs of a fork.

5. Transfer to the lined baking tray, make a slit in the center of each and brush with milk. Bake in the oven for about 25 minutes until golden and crisp. Best served warm.

Ingredients

1 Tbsp. vegetable oil
1 small onion, peeled and finely chopped
1 small carrot, peeled and finely chopped
1¼ cups (300 g) lean boneless lamb shoulder, finely chopped
1 Tbsp. freshly chopped thyme or 1 tsp. dried
salt and freshly ground black pepper
1½ Tbsp. flour
14 Tbsp. (200 ml) beef or lamb stock
2 Tbsp. whole milk, to glaze
1 quantity rough puff pastry or flaky pastry

A NOT SO HUMBLE PIE

Serves: 4–6   Preparation: 30 minutes plus cooling   Cooking: 3 hours 23 minutes

Venison has increased in popularity in recent years. Cooked slowly, its lean, melting texture makes a delicious alternative to beef.

1. First, make the filling. Put the venison in a bowl and toss in seasoning and flour. Melt the butter in a large saucepan until bubbling and add the meat along with any remaining flour. Cook, stirring, for about 5 minutes until browned all over. Remove from the pan using a slotted spoon and transfer to a heatproof plate.

2. Reheat the pan juices with the oil until bubbling, add the onion, carrot and celery to the saucepan and cook, stirring, for 3 minutes.

3. Return venison to the saucepan and add the juniper berries, sage, vinegar, and sugar. Stir in the wine. Bring to a boil, reduce to a simmer, cover, and cook gently for about 2 hours until tender. Allow to cool, discard the herbs, and transfer to a 7-cup (2.1-L) oval pie dish with rim—10 ¼ x 7½ x 3 inch (25½ x 19 x 7 cm). Push a pie funnel in the center. Preheat the oven to 425°F, (220°C, 200°C fan oven).

4. Roll out the pastry on a lightly floured surface to just larger than the pie dish. Make a hole in the center for the pie funnel. Carefully cut some of the excess pastry into thin strips and secure onto the edge of the pie dish with water. Brush with egg. Transfer the rolled out pastry to the top, trim, and press down onto the edge using a fork.

5. Roll out the pastry trimmings and cut out an antler design. Secure on top of the pie with beaten egg.

6. Put the dish on a baking tray, brush all over with beaten egg, and bake for 15 minutes; then, reduce the temperature to 375°F (190°C, 170°C fan oven) and cook for a further 50 minutes to 1 hour until crisp, golden, and hot—cover with foil if the pastry browns too quickly. Serve immediately.

Ingredients

4 cups (900 g) boneless shoulder of venison, trimmed and cut into 1 inch (2.5 cm) pieces
salt and freshly ground black pepper
4 Tbsp. flour
2 Tbsp. (25 g) butter
2 Tbsp. sunflower oil
1 red onion, peeled and chopped
1 large carrot, peeled and chopped
1 stick celery, trimmed and chopped
2 tsp. juniper berries, crushed
a few sprigs fresh sage tied with clean string
2 Tbsp. balsamic vinegar
2 Tbsp. dark brown sugar
¾ pt (450 ml) red wine
½ quantity puff pastry
1 egg, beaten, to glaze

VENISON AND VEGETABLE FILO LAYER

Serves: 4   Preparation: 30 minutes   Cooking: 50 minutes

Ingredients

14 Tbsp. (200 g) carrot,
   peeled and grated
14 Tbsp. (200 g) parsnip,
   peeled and grated
salt and freshly ground
   black pepper
1 cup (225 g) turnip or
   rutabaga (swede),
   peeled and grated
Pinch of grated nutmeg
2¼ cups (500 g) minced
   venison
1 medium leek, trimmed
   and shredded
2 Tbsp. freshly chopped
   rosemary or 2 tsp.
   dried
¼ cup (50 g) butter,
   melted
4 large sheets of filo
   pastry

If you're calorie counting, filo pastry is a great choice. You don't have to layer up the sheets with melted butter or margarine; beaten egg is a great alternative and gives a crisp, glossy finish. You can use any minced raw meat in this recipe.

1. Preheat the oven to 400°F (200°C, 180°C fan oven). Layer the carrot and parsnip in the bottom of a 12 x 7 x 1 ¼-inch (30 x 18 x 3 cm) rimless oval baking dish and season with salt and pepper. Top with the turnip or rutabaga (swede), season well, and sprinkle with nutmeg.

2. Mix the venison mince with the leek and plenty of seasoning and spoon evenly over the top of the vegetables. Mix the rosemary with the butter and spoon 2 tablespoons over the venison.

3. Lay the sheets of pastry on the work surface and brush with melted butter; then, scrunch up each sheet to make a loose "rosette" shape and arrange on top of the venison, making sure it is completely covered—pull the pastry rosettes apart again if necessary.

4. Stand the dish on a baking tray and brush with any remaining butter. Bake in the oven for about 50 minutes, until golden and cooked through—cover with foil if necessary to prevent the pastry from browning too quickly. Serve hot with freshly cooked vegetables or a crisp salad.

Variation

To use beaten egg instead of butter, mix all the rosemary into the venison mince and moisten the mixture with 3 tablespoons of beef stock. Follow the instructions in step 3 above using beaten egg instead of the butter.

PLOUGHMAN'S LUNCH

Makes: 8   Preparation: 40 minutes   Cooking: 40 minutes

Chunky and tasty, these pies are perfect for a picnic lunch, or, cut in halves or quarters, they make a delicious party snack. You can serve them straight out of the oven, but they have more flavor when cooled.

1. Preheat the oven to 400°F (200°C, 180°C fan oven). Put the pork, bacon, onion and pickle in a bowl and mix well. Season with pepper and set aside.

2. Make up the hot water crust pastry. Keep warm, cut off one quarter of the pastry, and keep covered separately.

3. Roll out the remaining pastry thinly on a lightly floured surface and cut out 6-inch (8 x 15 cm) rounds using a pastry cutter or upside down saucer, re-rolling as necessary. Gently press each circle into 4 inch (10 cm) diameter, 1½ inch (4 cm) deep rimless pie tins or molds. Then, put a portion of filling in each and pack down well. Sprinkle each with a layer of grated cheese.

4. Roll out the reserved pastry thinly and cut out 4-inch (8 x 10 cm) rounds, rerolling as necessary. Brush the inside of the pastry with egg and put a circle on top of each pie. Seal the edges together using the prongs of a fork. Make a hole in the center of each and brush the tops with egg.

5. Put the pies on a baking tray and bake in the oven for about 40 minutes until rich golden brown. Cool for 10 minutes and then loosen the edges with a round bladed knife and carefully remove from the tins. Serve hot or transfer to a wire rack to cool completely before serving.

Ingredients

- 1¾ cups (400 g) uncooked pork shoulder, ground
- 14 Tbsp. (200 g) rindless smoked streaky bacon, ground
- 1 onion, peeled and finely chopped
- 8 Tbsp. sandwich pickle freshly ground black pepper
- 10 Tbsp. (150 g) mature cheddar cheese, grated
- 1 quantity hot water crust pastry
- 1 egg, beaten, to glaze

PARTY SLICE

Serves: 10–12   Preparation: 50 minutes plus cooling   Cooking: 1 hour 30 minutes

In days gone by, no self-respecting buffet table would have been complete without this classic sliced pie. Nowadays, we've got so many other choices to offer our guests, it's often overlooked. Traditionally made with minced veal, I prefer to use pork or chicken. It does take a while to make, but it's guaranteed to impress.

1. Preheat the oven to 400°F (200°C, 180°C fan oven). Grease the base and sides of a 11 x 4 x 3-inch (28 x 10 x 7.5 cm) terrine dish. Put the ham, bacon, and minced meat in a bowl and mix in the sage, salt, plenty of pepper, and nutmeg. Set aside.

2. Cut off one quarter of the pastry and keep warm. Roll out the remaining pastry thinly on a lightly floured surface to form a rectangle approximately 16 x 10 inch (40 x 25 cm) and gently press into the dish, right to the top. Trim and reserve the excess pastry.

3. Pack one third of the meat into the pastry case and lay the eggs upright and evenly spaced down the center. Pack the remaining meat mixture around and over the eggs. Brush the inside edge of the pastry with egg.

4. Roll out the reserved pastry to fit exactly inside the top of the tin and press down on top of the meat. Pinch the two edges of pastry together all around the top to seal. Make a ½-inch (1 cm) hole in the center of the lid and place a large piping nozzle, pointed side down, in the hole.

5. If you like, roll out the trimmings, cut out your design and use to decorate the top of the pie, securing on the pastry lid using beaten egg.

Ingredients

1¾ cups (400 g) uncooked smoked ham gammon, ground
½ cup (115 g) rindless smoked streaky bacon, ground
1 cup, 10 Tbsp. (375 g) lean uncooked ground pork, chicken, or veal
2 Tbsp. freshly chopped sage or 2 tsp. dried
1¼ tsp. salt
freshly ground black pepper
½ tsp. ground nutmeg
1 quantity hot water crust pastry made with bread (strong plain) flour
4 cold hard boiled eggs, peeled
1 egg, beaten, to glaze
4 sheets fine leaf gelatin
approximately 1 cup 2 Tbsp. (250 ml) cold good quality weak or low salt chicken stock

6. Put the dish on a baking tray and glaze the top with egg. Bake for 30 minutes and then reduce the temperature to 375°F (190°C, 170°C fan oven) and cook for a further 1 hour until richly golden—cover with foil if it browns too quickly. Stand for 15 minutes.

7. Meanwhile, cut the gelatin into small pieces and place in a heatproof jug. Add the stock and leave aside to soak for 10 minutes. Place the jug over a pan of simmering water until the gelatin has melted. Mix well.

8. Gradually pour the gelatin through the nozzle into the hot pie, allowing the gelatin to settle after each pour, stopping when the pie ceases to absorb any more. Remove the nozzle and allow to cool and then chill overnight. The next day, release the pie from the tin; using a large serrated knife, cut into slices. Best enjoyed at room temperature.

OLD FASHIONED EGG AND BACON PIE

Serves: 6   Preparation: 35 minutes   Cooking: 34 minutes

Another of my pies from yesteryear. This one reminds me of tea at my Granny's. Use good quality, fresh eggs for the tastiest filling and chunky smoked bacon, but you can use unsmoked if you prefer. This pie tastes great cold, but I prefer it when it's been out of the oven for about a half hour and still warm.

1. Preheat the oven to 400°F (200°C, 180°C fan oven). Roll out ⅔ of the pastry on a lightly floured work surface to fit a 9½ x 1 ¼ inch (24 x 3½ cm) round, 1¼ inch (3½ cm) deep pie tin or dish with rim. Carefully fit the pastry to the dish and rim, neaten the edges, and place on a baking tray. Set aside.

2. Put the bacon in a frying pan and dry fry for 3–4 minutes until sealed all over. Drain on kitchen paper. Set aside.

3. Break the eggs into a jug and beat together until well blended. Stir in the cream or milk, chives if using, salt, and plenty of black pepper.

4. Roll out the remaining pastry thinly to make a rectangle about 10 inch (25 cm) long, and cut into ½ inch (1 cm) wide strips. Interlace the pastry strips on a round piece of baking parchment, pressing them gently together to seal.

5. Put the bacon in the pastry base and pour the beaten egg mixture over it. Brush the pastry edge with a little water. Carefully lift the pastry lattice on the paper and flip or slide on top of the pie. Peel away the paper, press the ends of the pastry strips to the edge of the pie dish, and trim to neaten.

6. Bake for 15 minutes. Reduce the oven temperature to 350°F (180°C, 160°C fan oven) and cook for a further 15 minutes until the pastry and egg filling set. Serve hot or cold accompanied with crisp salad.

Ingredients

¾ quantity of shortcrust pastry
1 cup 1 Tbsp. (250 g) thickly sliced, rindless, smoked back bacon, chopped
4 eggs
1½ cups (450 ml) single cream or whole milk
2 Tbsp. freshly chopped chives, optional
1 tsp. salt
freshly ground black pepper

MINI PORK AND CHORIZO PICNIC PIES

Makes: 12   Preparation: 30 minutes   Cooking: 30 minutes

Ingredients

7 Tbsp. (100 g) ground pork
7 Tbsp. (100 g) chorizo, skinned and finely chopped or minced
2 garlic cloves, peeled and crushed
3 Tbsp. red pesto
1½ tsp. smoked paprika
freshly ground black pepper
½ quantity whole wheat or spelt shortcrust pastry
1 egg, beaten, to glaze

Small, savory pies ideal for packed lunch boxes or party food. Use minced chicken instead of pork, or replace the chorizo with minced bacon for a less spicy snack.

1. Preheat the oven to 400°F (200°C, 180°C fan oven). Put the pork and bacon in a bowl and mix in the garlic, pesto, and smoked paprika. Season with pepper and set aside.

2. Roll out the pastry thinly on a lightly floured surface. Using a 3½ inch (9 cm) round pastry cutter, stamp out 9 circles, reserving the trimmings. Gently press each circle into 2¾ inch (7 cm) diameter, ¾ inch (2 cm) deep bun tins. Put a portion of filling in each and pack down well to just below the pastry rim. Brush the exposed pastry with water.

3. Roll out the trimmings thinly and stamp out 2¼-inch (9 x 6-cm) rounds, rerolling as necessary. Press a circle of pastry on top of each pie and seal the edges using the prongs of a fork. Make a hole in the center of each and brush the tops with egg.

4. Bake in the oven for about 30 minutes until rich golden brown. Cool for 10 minutes before carefully removing from the tins and transferring to a wire rack. Serve warm or allow to cool completely. Delicious with tangy tomato and chilli chutney

Variation

For an extra rich version of these pies, use the same quantity of double cheese pastry.

SAUSAGE AND APPLE PLAIT

Serves: 4   Preparation: 25 minutes   Cooking: 40 minutes

This is a giant sausage roll with an impressive folded pastry top. Leave out the apple if you prefer.

1. Preheat the oven to 400°F (200°C, 180°C fan oven). Line a large baking tray with baking parchment. Put the sausage meat in a bowl and mix in the sage and onion. Set aside.

2. On a lightly floured surface, roll out the pastry into a rectangle 12 x 8 inches (30 x 20 cm) and spread the sausage meat evenly down the center. Flatten the meat to a depth of 1inch keeping it ¾ inch (2 cm) from either short end.

3. Halve and thinly slice the apple and then arrange the slices, overlapping, all over the sausage meat. Season well.

4. Make 8 slanting cuts in the pastry to within ½ inch (1 cm) of the filling at 1 inch (2½ cm) intervals on either side of the filling. Fold the end pieces of pastry in and around the ends of sausage meat to cover it.

5. Take a strip from each side and cross over the filling all down the length of the sausagemeat to give a plaited effect, sealing with a little egg on top.

6. Carefully transfer to the lined baking tray. Brush all over with egg, sprinkle with poppy seeds, and bake in the oven for about 40 minutes until golden and cooked through. Serve hot or cold in slices, with mustard.

Ingredients

2 cups (450 g) good quality pork sausage meat
3 Tbsp. freshly chopped sage or 2 tsp. dried
1 small onion, peeled and finely chopped
½ quantity rough puff pastry
1 small pink or red-skinned eating apple, cored, halved, and thinly sliced
salt and freshly ground black pepper
1 egg, beaten, to glaze
2 tsp. poppy seeds

Variations

For a simple sweet "plait," replace the sausagemeat with a combination of fruity mincemeat and grated marzipan (if preferred) and pop the apple on top as described above. For more indulgence, use puff pastry. Best served warm with cream.

Pulled Pork and Char-Grilled Veg Pie

Serves: 4–6   Preparation: 25 minutes plus cooling   Cooking: 1 hour

Ingredients

1 each red and yellow peppers, deseeded and thickly sliced

1 large zucchini (courgette), trimmed, halved, and sliced diagonally

1 red onion, peeled and cut into thick slices

2 Tbsp. olive oil

1 Tbsp. freshly chopped thyme or 1 tsp. dried

salt and freshly ground black pepper

1½ cups (350 g) cold "pulled pork"—see aside—or other cooked meat

8 Tbsp. sweet tomato chutney

2 tsp. smoked paprika

½ quantity rough puff pastry

1 egg, beaten, to glaze

a few small sprigs fresh thyme

A pie based on an American recipe for cooking pork very slowly. It requires some planning if you're starting from scratch but is a great way to use up leftovers. Slow cooked pork is one of my favorite meats, and it retains its succulence on reheating, so it is perfect for pie making. Serve this simply with coleslaw and salad.

1. Preheat the grill to a medium/hot setting. Line the grill pan with foil. Put the vegetables in a bowl and toss in the oil, chopped thyme, and seasoning. Spread out evenly in the grill pan. Cook, turning occasionally, for 15 minutes until tender and lightly charred. Leave to cool.

2. Preheat the oven to 400°F (200°C, 180°C fan oven). Put the cold vegetables in the bottom of a 8 ¾ x 6 x 2-inch (22 x 15 x 5-cm) oblong pie dish with rim. Season well and put the pork on top. Mix the chutney and paprika together and spoon over the top.

3. Roll out the pastry thinly on a lightly floured surface to just larger than the pie dish. Cut some of the excess pastry into thin strips and secure onto the edge of the pie dish with water. Brush with egg. Transfer the rolled out pastry to the top, trim, and press down onto the edge using a fork. Put the dish on a baking tray.

4. Make a hole in the center of the pie and brush all over with egg. Sprinkle with a few sprigs of thyme. Bake in the oven for about 45 minutes until risen, golden, and piping hot. Best served hot or warm, with coleslaw and salad.

To make "pulled pork" (serves 4–6)

Put a large roasting pan of water in the bottom of the oven and then preheat the oven to 240°F (120°C, 100°C fan oven). Wash and pat dry a 3 lb 5 oz (1½ kg) boneless pork shoulder joint (with skin on). Remove any string and rub all over with 2 tablespoons olive oil. Heat a large frying pan until hot, add the pork, and cook for 5 minutes, turning it to seal all over. Drain and place in a roasting pan. Mix 2 teaspoons smoked paprika with 2 teaspoons dried oregano and plenty of salt and pepper. Rub all over the pork and cook in the oven for 3 hours. Remove the tray of water, baste the pork, and continue to cook for a further 3 hours at least, basting occasionally, or until falling apart. Strip away the skin and fat and "pull" the cooked pork meat apart into shreds using two forks. Serve hot or cold.

MUTTON PIE

Serves: 4   Preparation: 40 minutes plus cooling   Cooking: 3 hours 20 minutes

Ingredients

2 Tbsp. vegetable oil
2 tsp. cumin seeds,
    roasted and lightly
    crushed
2 tsp. coriander, roasted
    and lightly crushed
6½ cups, 2 Tbsp. (1½ kg)
    mutton or lamb shanks,
    trimmed
2 Tbsp. (25 g) butter
1 onion, peeled and
    chopped
2 Tbsp. flour
2 cups 2 Tbsp. (500 ml)
    chicken stock
2 cups (450 g) cooked
    diced potato
1 cup (225 g) cooked
    diced carrot
1 quantity suet crust
    pastry made up with 2
    tbsp freshly chopped
    rosemary or 2 tsp dried
1 egg, beaten, to glaze
rosemary to garnish

Mutton today it is quite difficult to get hold of and expensive. It's my favorite meat for flavor, but lamb shanks make a good substitute.

1. Heat the oil in a large saucepan and cook the seeds with the shanks for about 5 minutes, turning in the oil, to seal it all over. Transfer to a heatproof plate using tongs, reserving the cooking juices in the pan.

2. Reheat the juices with the butter until bubbling and cook the onion, stirring, for 5 minutes until softened; then, stir in the flour to make a paste. Gradually stir in the stock and bring to a boil, stirring constantly, and simmer for 5 minutes.

3. Return the shanks to the pan, cover with a tight-fitting lid and reduce to a gentle simmer. Cook for about 2 hours, turning the shanks occasionally, or until very tender. Reserving the cooking gravy, take the lamb off the bones in chunky pieces and place in a 5½-cup (1.65-L) oval pie dish with rim. Mix in the potato and carrot and pour the gravy on top. Leave to cool.

4. Preheat the oven to 425°F (220°C, 200°C fan oven). Push the bones in if using or place a pie funnel in the middle. Roll out the pastry on a lightly floured surface to just larger than the pie dish. Make small crosses in the pastry for the bones or pie funnel. Carefully cut some of the excess pastry into thin strips and secure onto the edge of the pie dish with water. Brush with egg.

5. Transfer the rolled pastry to the top of the dish, trim to neaten, and press carefully down onto the edge using your thumb. Cover the bones with foil to prevent them from burning. Brush the pastry with egg.

6. Put the dish on a baking tray and bake for 10 minutes and then reduce the temperature to 350°F (180°C, 160°C fan oven) and cook for a further 50 minutes to 1 hour until golden and the meat is piping hot—cover with foil if the pastry browns too quickly. Garnish with rosemary and serve immediately.

SPEHA

Makes: 12   Preparation: 30 minutes   Cooking: 33 minutes

Middle Eastern food is never far off my radar; I love the fragrant spices used throughout the region. These Lebanese open lamb and tomato pies are made with a special type of pastry dough, but I use filo for my version, and top with pomegranate seeds to add crunch.

1. Preheat the oven to 400°F (200°C, 180°C fan oven). Lightly grease a large baking tray with some of the melted butter. Heat a frying pan until hot and then add the pine nuts and stir 2–3 minutes until golden brown. Drain on kitchen paper and set aside to cool.

2. Place the onion in a bowl and mix in the garlic, spices, lamb, molasses or lemon juice, chopped tomato, and pine nuts. Season well and mix together until well combined. Divide into 12 equally sized pieces and form into round burger shapes approximately 2 inches (5 cm) in diameter.

3. Taking one sheet of filo at a time, brush all over with butter and then fold the bottom third up. Brush with butter and fold the top third down. Using a 4-inch (10-cm) cutter, stamp out 3 rounds. Repeat with the other 3 sheets to give you 12 filo rounds in total. Discard the trimmings and brush with butter.

4. Divide the lamb mixture between the circles and then pinch the rounds together at the four corners, bringing up the sides to make a case around the filling but leaving the top open.

5. Arrange the pies on the baking tray and bake for 25–30 minutes until golden brown. Serve hot or warm, sprinkled with pomegranate seeds.

Sumac

Sumac is a powdered spice and key ingredient in many Middle Eastern dishes. It has a powerful, tart, citrusy flavor; a little goes a long way.

Ingredients

¼ cup (50 g) butter, melted
2 Tbsp. (25 g) pine nuts
1 small red onion, peeled and finely chopped
1 garlic clove, peeled and crushed
½ tsp. ground allspice
½ tsp. ground sumac— see below
1 cup 2 Tbsp. (250 g) lean lamb mince
1 tsp. pomegranate molasses or 1 Tbsp. freshly squeezed lemon juice
1 large ripe tomato, cored and finely chopped
salt and freshly ground black pepper
4 large sheets filo pastry, at least 12 inches (30 cm) long
2 Tbsp. fresh pomegranate seeds

CHURDLES

Makes: 8   Preparation: 30 minutes plus cooling   Cooking: 27 minutes

Ingredients

5 Tbsp. (75 g) unsalted butter

1 small onion, peeled and finely chopped

¼ cup (50 g) smoked rindless streaky bacon, finely chopped

¾ cup (175 g) prepared lambs' liver, finely chopped

1 Tbsp freshly chopped sage or 1 tsp. dried

salt and freshly ground black pepper

2 Tbsp. (25 g) fresh white breadcrumbs

1 quantity shortcrust pastry

1 egg, beaten, to glaze

I spent my later school days in West Sussex, and I can honestly say I never came across a churdle until I started working in London. These traditional yet relatively unknown mitre-shaped pies are unusual in that they have a lambs' liver filling.

1. Melt 2 tablespoons (25 g) of the butter in a frying pan until bubbling and then gently fry the onion and bacon for 5 minutes to soften but not brown. Add the liver and cook gently, stirring, for 1–2 minutes to seal the liver all over. Remove from the heat and stir in the sage, plenty of seasoning, and the breadcrumbs to make a stuffing mixture. Set aside to cool.

2. To make the pies, preheat the oven to 400°F (200°C, 180°C fan oven). Line a large baking tray with baking parchment. Divide the pastry into 2 equal portions and roll out each on a lightly floured surface to form 9½-inch (24-cm) squares and then cut each into 4.

3. Divide the filling between each square. Cut the remaining butter into 8 small pieces and dot on top of the filling and brush the edges with water. Working on one at a time, bring up the sides, pinching the edges together in the middle to make a mitre-shaped parcel.

4. Transfer the pies to the lined baking tray and brush all over with egg. Bake in the oven for about 20 minutes until golden. Best served warm.

Variation

Some recipes mix grated cheese into the filling. If you want to try it, add 5 tablespoons (75 g) grated mature cheddar into the cold filling before putting onto the pastry squares.

POULTRY

B'STILLA

Serves: 6   Preparation: 45 minutes plus cooling   Cooking: 55 minutes

Ingredients

3 prepared squabs
    or wood pigeons,
    approximately
    1 lb 5 oz (600 g) weight
a small bunch each of
    parsley and cilantro
    (coriander)
1 stick cinnamon
salt and freshly ground
    black pepper
1 onion, peeled and finely
    chopped
10 Tbsp. (150 g) butter
4 large eggs, beaten
¼ cup. (50 g) flaked
    almonds
¼ cup (50 g) sultanas
4 Tbsp. freshly chopped
    cilantro (coriander)
6 large sheets filo pastry,
    at least 12 inches (30
    cm) long, thawed if
    frozen
2 tsp. confectioner's
    (icing) sugar
1½ tsp. ground cinnamon

Pronounced "bas-tee-ya," I had this on my very first trip to Morocco, and have enjoyed making my own version ever since. I'm going back to the traditional filling which uses pigeon, but you can use 1¼ cups (300 g) cooked chicken (brown meat is best) or duck. The sugar dusting sounds a bit weird, but it really works.

1. Wash and pat dry the squabs or pigeons and place breast side down in a saucepan to which they fit snugly side by side. Add the herbs, cinnamon, seasoning, onion and ¼ cup (50 g) butter. Pour sufficient water to barely cover the pigeons. Bring to a boil and then cover and simmer very gently for 1 hour. Turn off the heat and allow to cool. Drain the birds, reserving the liquid. Discard the skin and carefully strip the meat from the bones and set aside.

2. Strain the cooking liquid into another saucepan and bring to a boil. Cook rapidly for about 10 minutes to reduce by half. Remove from the heat and immediately whisk in the eggs; then, return to a very low heat and stir for about 10 minutes until thickened like a light custard. Season to taste and set aside.

3. Meanwhile, melt 2 tablespoons (25 g) butter until bubbling and gently fry the almonds for 4–5 minutes, stirring, until they turn golden. Drain on kitchen paper and set aside.

4. Preheat the oven to 400°F (200°C, 180°C fan oven). Melt the remaining butter. Brush a 8-inch (20-cm) round spring form cake pan with butter and cover the base with 2 overlapping sheets of pastry, leaving the edges overhanging the pan. Brush with butter and continue layering with the remaining sheets, brushing each with butter and leaving the edges overhanging, making sure the pan is evenly lined. Put the cooked meat in the bottom of the pan, scatter with almonds, sultanas, and chopped cilantro. Pour the egg mixture over the meat mixture.

5. Fold the overhanging pastry over the filling, piece by piece, brushing with butter as you go, and then brush the top with any remaining butter and place the pan on a baking tray. Cook for 30 minutes until crisp and golden; then, turn out, upside down, onto a baking tray lined with baking parchment and return to the oven to cook for a further 10 minutes.

6. Carefully slide onto a warm serving plate. Dust the top with confectioner's (icing) sugar and lay thin strips of baking parchment in a lattice pattern on top. Dust lightly with cinnamon and carefully remove the paper strips. Serve warm.

GOLDEN CHICKEN PIE

Serves: 6-8   Preparation: 40 minutes plus cooling   Cooking: 2 hours 30 minutes

Cold pressed rapeseed oil is truly delicious, very golden, and nutritious to boot; I'm a complete convert.

1. Place the chicken breast side down in a saucepan to fit snugly. Add 1 onion, carrot, celery, and bay leaves. Pour over sufficient water to barely cover the chicken. Bring to a boil and then cover and simmer very gently for 1½ hours until tender and cooked through. Turn off the heat and cool.

2. Drain the chicken and carrot (strain the cooking liquid and use as stock) and discard the other vegetables and bay leaves. Discard the chicken skin and carefully strip the meat from the bones. Cut into bite-sized pieces along with the carrot and put in a large bowl. Cover and chill until required.

3. Meanwhile, chop the remaining onion. Heat the oil until hot and then gently fry the garlic and onion for 7–8 minutes until tender and lightly golden. Set aside to cool.

4. To assemble the pie, preheat the oven to 400°F (200°C, 180°C fan oven). Mix the sweet corn kernels, cream, and creamed sweet corn into the chicken and carrot along with seasoning. Stir in the onion mixture. Spoon into 10 x 8 x 2-inch (25 x 20 x 5-cm) pie dish and push a pie funnel in the center if preferred.

5. Roll out the pastry as thinly as possible—it may crack, so simply patch together. Using a 3½-inch (9-cm) round cutter, stamp out 9 circles, rerolling as necessary. If using a pie funnel, cut one circle in half. Lightly roll each piece of pastry a little more to make it slightly bigger.

6. Arrange the rounds, overlapping, all over the dish—put the 2 halves on either side of the pie funnel if using. Stand the dish on a baking tray, brush with beaten egg, and sprinkle with cornmeal. Bake in the oven for about 1 hour until golden and piping hot. Serve immediately.

Ingredients

- 6½ cups, 2 Tbsp. (1½ kg) corn-fed, oven-ready chicken, washed and dried
- 2 onions, peeled
- 1 large carrot, peeled and roughly chopped
- 2 sticks celery, trimmed and roughly chopped
- 2 bay leaves
- 1 Tbsp. cold pressed rapeseed oil
- 2 garlic cloves, peeled and crushed
- 1 cup 2 Tbsp. (250 g) cooked sweetcorn kernels
- 6 Tbsp. double cream
- 15 oz (418 g) can cream style sweet corn
- salt and freshly ground black pepper
- ½ quantity oil pastry, made up using cold pressed rapeseed oil
- 1 egg, beaten, to glaze
- 1 Tbsp. fine ground cornmeal

UPPER CRUST GUINEA FOWL AND GRAPE PIE

Serves: 4   Preparation: 30 minutes plus cooling   Cooking: 1 hour

Ingredients

1 oven-ready guinea fowl, quartered (or chicken)
salt and freshly ground black pepper
2 Tbsp. (25 g) flour
2 Tbsp. (25 g) unsalted butter
2 Tbsp. olive oil
2 shallots, peeled and finely chopped
1 clove garlic, peeled and finely chopped
½ cup (150 ml) dry white wine
14 Tbsp. (200 ml) chicken stock
1 bay leaf
4 Tbsp. heavy cream
¾ cup (175 g) seedless green grapes, washed
2 Tbsp. freshly chopped tarragon
½ quantity puff pastry
1 egg, beaten, to glaze

Based on the retro dish Chicken Veronique, this tasty dish should impress your guests, and the puff pastry lid has the "wow" factor alone. No precooking and cooling required; this one's ready to serve immediately.

1. Wash and pat dry the guinea fowl. Season the flour well and dust all over the meat. In a deep frying pan with a lid, melt the butter with the oil until bubbling and then fry the guinea fowl for about 10 minutes, turning occasionally, until golden all over. Drain, reserving the pan juices, and put on a heatproof plate.

2. Reheat the pan juices and gently fry the shallot and garlic for 5 minutes until softened but not browned and then gradually stir in the wine and stock. Add the bay leaf and replace the guinea fowl in the pan. Bring to a boil, cover and simmer gently for about 30 minutes. Stir in the cream, grapes, and tarragon and continue to cook for a further 5 minutes until tender and cooked through. Discard the bay leaf. Transfer to the heatproof serving dish of your choice and keep warm.

3. Meanwhile, preheat the oven to 425°F (220°C, 200°C fan oven). Line a baking tray with baking parchment. On a lightly floured surface, roll out the pastry to make a rectangle approximately 10 x 9 inches (25 x 23 cm).

4. Carefully transfer the pastry to the tray and score in a diagonal criss-cross design using a sharp knife. Brush with egg. Bake in the oven for 12–15 minutes until golden and risen.

5. To serve, carefully transfer the pastry lid to the top of your serving dish and serve up immediately—you may find it easier to put the pastry on a cutting board to divide up the pastry. Accompany the pie with freshly cooked vegetables or crusty bread and crisp salad.

CHRISTMAS CRANBERRY TURKEY PIE

Serves: 6–8   Preparation: 40 minutes plus cooling   Cooking: 1 hour

Here is a great way to use up leftover Christmas meat. This recipe is essentially a pastry case baked, cooled, and ready to fill with a tasty chilled filling. If you don't want to make a white sauce, you can use a combination of reduced fat mayonnaise and yogurt.

1. Preheat the oven to 400°F (200°C, 180°C fan oven). Grease and line an 8 inch (20 cm) diameter, 1¾ inch (4 cm) deep spring form cake tin. On a lightly floured surface, roll out the pastry quite thickly to fit the tin and transfer the pastry inside. Trim and reserve the trimmings.

2. Push a circle of baking parchment into the pastry case and fill to three quarters with baking beans or lentils or rice. Place the tin on a baking tray and blind bake for 20 minutes.

3. Remove the beans or rice and paper and remove the pastry from the tin. Put on a baking tray, prick the base with a fork, and brush inside and out with egg. Bake for a further 20 minutes until richly golden. Cool on a wire rack.

4. Meanwhile, roll out the trimmings thinly and cut out a 4 ¼-inch (11-cm) star shape. Place on a lightly greased baking tray, prick lightly with a fork, and brush with beaten egg. Bake for 12–15 minutes until golden. Transfer to a wire rack to cool.

5. For the filling, melt the butter in a saucepan. Add the flour and cook for 1 minute. Remove from heat and gradually stir in the milk. Add the bay leaf, cloves, and nutmeg. Return to heat and cook, stirring, until boiling; then, simmer for 2 minutes. Remove from heat, stir in the cream, 2 tablespoons of parsley, and seasoning. Set aside to cool. Discard the bay leaf and cloves.

Ingredients

½ quantity hot water crust pastry
Baking beans, lentils, or rice
1 egg, beaten, to glaze
2 Tbsp. (25 g) butter
2 Tbsp. (25 g) flour
1 cup (300 ml) whole milk
1 bay leaf
4 cloves
pinch of grated nutmeg
¼ cup (50 ml) heavy cream
3 Tbsp. freshly chopped parsley
salt and freshly ground black pepper
½ cup (115 g) prepared cranberries, thawed if frozen
2 Tbsp. water
¼ cup (50 g) superfine (castor) sugar
½ cup (115 g) cooked turkey meat, finely chopped or minced
½ cup (115 g) cooked ham, finely chopped or minced

6. Put the cranberries in a small saucepan and add 2 tablespoons of water. Heat gently until steaming and then simmer for about 3 minutes until the berries begin to soften. Remove from the heat and stir in the sugar. Leave to cool.

7. To assemble the pie, put the pastry case on a serving plate. Put the turkey and ham in a bowl. Mix in the sauce and season to taste. Spoon into the pastry case and top with the cranberry mixture. Either serve immediately at room temperature or chill for an hour before serving. Sprinkle with remaining parsley to garnish.

COCK-A-LEEKIE CHEESY PIE

Serves: 4–6   Preparation: 35 minutes plus cooling   Cooking: 55 minutes

A tasty dish for cheese lovers, this top-only pie makes a good supper dish or light lunch. Use blue cheese if you prefer and add some finely chopped celery to the leeks for extra savor.

1. Melt half the butter in a frying pan until bubbling and stir fry the leeks for 5 minutes until softened. Set aside to cool.

2. Meanwhile, melt the remaining butter in a saucepan, add the flour, and cook for 1 minute. Remove from the heat and gradually stir in the milk. Return to the heat and cook, stirring, until boiling point is reached; then, simmer for 2 minutes. Remove from the heat, stir in the cheese, season to taste, lay a piece of buttered greaseproof paper on the sauce, and set aside to cool.

3. To make up the pie, preheat the oven to 400°F (200°C, 180°C fan oven). Put the chicken in a bowl and mix in the cold leek and sauce. Season as necessary and then spoon into a 8-inch (20-cm) round pie dish with rim, 1¾ inch (4 cm) deep.

4. Roll out the pastry thinly on a lightly floured surface to form an approximately 8 ¾-inch (22-cm) circle. Cut the edges off the pastry to neaten and use these pieces to line the edge of the pie dish, securing them onto the dish with water. Cut the remaining pastry into 12–14 strips.

5. Arrange the strips gently on top of the filling in a diagonal criss-cross pattern—6 or 7 one way and the remaining in the other direction—and then interlace the strips. Once in place, secure them onto the pastry edge with beaten egg and trim the edge to neaten.

6. Put the pie on a baking tray, brush with egg, and bake for 25 minutes. Reduce the temperature to 350°F (180°C, 160°C fan oven) and cook for a further 20–25 minutes until golden and hot. Serve immediately.

Ingredients

¼ cup (50 g) butter
1 large leeks, trimmed and shredded
2 Tbsp. (25 g) flour
1 cup (300 ml) whole milk
10 Tbsp. (150 g) mature Cheddar cheese, grated
salt and freshly ground black pepper
1¼ cup (300 g) cooked chicken meat, cut into bite-sized pieces
½ quantity double cheese pastry
1 egg, beaten, to glaze

Topsy-Turvy
Roast Dinner Pie

Serves: 6   Preparation: 20 minutes plus cooling   Cooking: 40 minutes

Ingredients

1 Tbsp. vegetable oil
6 baby onion or shallots, peeled and halved
4 rashers rindless streaky bacon, chopped
1 Tbsp. freshly chopped sage or 1 tsp. dried
1 cup (225 g) cooked chicken, cut into chunky pieces
12 cooked cocktail sausages or pieces of cooked sausage
6 pieces sage and onion stuffing (packet mix or leftover)
salt and freshly ground black pepper
½ quantity flaky or rough puff pastry
1 egg, beaten, to glaze
fresh sage to garnish

I first made this one Boxing Day with the trimmings left over from the previous day's dinner. Everyone enjoyed it, and it's now become a family favorite. Of course, it works with any roast dinner leftovers, so you can make up your own combinations.

1. Heat the oil in a 10-inch (25-cm), round, flameproof, and ovenproof dish and gently fry the onions and bacon for 5 minutes, stirring, until softened. Remove from the heat, sprinkle with sage, and cool for 20 minutes.

2. To make up the pie, preheat the oven to 400°F (200°C, 180°C fan oven). Arrange the chicken pieces, sausages, and stuffing evenly in the dish and season.

3. Roll out the pastry on a lightly floured surface to a diameter just slightly bigger all around than the dish and place it over the top. Brush with egg and fold over the edges to neaten. Prick lightly with a fork and bake in the oven for about 35 minutes until golden and puffed up. Stand for 10 minutes and then carefully invert onto a large, warmed serving platter. Serve immediately, garnished with sage and accompanied with cranberry sauce.

Variations

- Add pieces of cooked roast vegetable to the pan if you have some left over. Keep the different ingredients about the same size so that the pastry fits neatly on top.

- For a sweet version, gently fry slices of apple, pear, or peach in butter. Scatter with sugar and top with puff pastry. Bake as above. Best served warm with clotted cream or vanilla ice cream.

PHEASANT, PARSNIP, AND RED CURRANT PUFFS

Serves: 4   Preparation: 30 minutes   Cooking: 1 hour 10 minutes

A special occasion pie that is ideal for an autumnal evening get-together or Sunday lunch. The pastry top is cooked separately, so you can either serve your filling immediately or reheat it to serve.

1. Wash and pat dry the pheasant pieces and season all over. Melt the butter in a large saucepan until bubbling and fry the bacon and onion for 5 minutes until softened. Add the pheasant and cook, turning in the butter, for about 5 minutes until sealed all over, reserving the pan juices. Remove the pheasant from the pan and put on a heatproof plate.

2. Blend the flour into the cooking juices and then add the stock and wine. Add the allspice, red currant jelly, and parsnips. Bring to a boil, stirring, and then return the pheasant to the pan and cover. Reduce to a gentle simmer and cook for about 1 hour until tender and cooked through.

3. Meanwhile, make the pastry lids. Preheat the oven to 425°F (220°C, 200°C fan oven). Line a baking tray with baking parchment. On a lightly floured board, roll out the pastry to a 10-inch (25-cm) square and divide into 4 equal portions. Score the tops diagonally with a knife and knock up the edges.

4. Transfer the pastry to the lined tray and brush with egg. Bake in the oven for about 20 minutes until golden and puffy. Keep warm.

5. To serve, take the pheasant meat off the bones if preferred and spoon portions onto warm serving plates. Sit a pastry puff on top, garnish, and serve immediately with vegetables.

Ingredients

4 cups (2 lb, 2 x 900 g) oven ready pheasant, skinned and quartered

salt and freshly ground black pepper

2 Tbsp. (25g) butter

4 pieces rindless smoked streaky bacon, chopped

1 onion, peeled and chopped

3 Tbsp. flour

1½ cups (450 ml) game or chicken stock

½ cup (150 ml) red wine

½ tsp. ground allspice

4 Tbsp. red currant jelly

1½ cups (250 g) parsnips, peeled and diced

½ quantity puff pastry

1 egg, beaten, to glaze

red currants and parsley to garnish

Variations

If you want to make the pheasant filling in advance, simply cool, cover, and refrigerate for up to 48 hours. Turn into a saucepan, cover, and reheat gently for about 40 minutes, stirring occasionally, until piping hot.

CHICKEN PITHVIERS

Makes: 4   Preparation: 30 minutes plus cooling   Cooking: 38minutes

Ingredients

3 Tbsp. (40 g) butter
1 small onion, peeled and
    chopped
2 Tbsp. (25 g) flaked
    almonds
¼ cup (50 g) cooked
    basmati rice
½ cup (115 g) cooked
    chicken, finely
    chopped
3 Tbsp. (40 g) sultanas
1 tsp. ground cinnamon
4 Tbsp. freshly chopped
    cilantro (coriander)
salt and freshly ground
    black pepper
1 quantity puff pastry
1 egg, beaten, to glaze

Gâteau pithviers is a traditional, rich French puff pastry and almond dessert. I thought the idea could work with a savory filling, and I've put together some ingredients with a hint of Moroccan spice that transforms a sweet into a main course.

1. Preheat the oven to 400°F (200°C, 180°C fan oven). Line a large baking tray with baking parchment. Melt 2 tablespoons (25 g) of the butter in a frying pan until bubbling and then gently fry the onion for 5 minutes. Add the flaked almonds and continue to cook, stirring, for a further 2–3 minutes until the almonds are lightly golden. Cool for 10 minutes.

2. Put the rice and chicken in a bowl and mix in the sultanas, cinnamon, and cilantro. Season well and stir in the oniony almond mixture.

3. Divide the pastry in half, and on a lightly floured surface, roll out each piece of pastry thinly to form a 12-inch (30-cm) square. Using an upside down saucer or round cutter, cut out 6 inch (15 cm) circles from each square.

4. Arrange 4 circles on the lined baking tray and divide the chicken mixture between each round. Spread the filling to within ¾ inch (2 cm) of the edge of the pastry. Dot each with a piece of the remaining butter.

5. Brush the pastry edge with beaten egg and place another round of pastry on top. Press the top down over the filling and knock up the edges to seal.

6. Score the tops lightly in a spiral pattern and brush with egg. Bake for about 30 minutes until golden and puffed up. Best served warm.

Variations
For a veggie version, replace the chicken with cooked mushrooms, cashew nuts, almonds, or pistachios.

Gram Pastry with Curried Turkey

Serves: 6   Preparation: 40 minutes plus cooling   Cooking: 1 hour 20 minutes

I love the beany, earthy flavor of chickpea flour; it's delicious with Indian flavors and bakes to a lovely golden color too. It is best mixed with another flour to make it easier to work with. I use buckwheat to make the pie completely gluten-free, but you can use spelt or another wheat flour if preferred.

1. Dust the work surface lightly with gram flour and roll out two thirds of the pastry to fit a 8¾-inch (22-cm) diameter rimless pie dish, 1¼-inch (3-cm) deep. Transfer the pastry to the dish and press together any cracks. Trim to neaten the edges. Wrap the remaining pastry and chill along with the pastry case for at least 30 minutes.

2. Meanwhile, heat the oil in a saucepan and gently fry the onion and garlic for 5 minutes. Stir in the curry paste and turkey and cook for a further 15 minutes, stirring, until the turkey is sealed all over.

3. Add the chopped tomatoes, bring to a boil, cover, and simmer for 15 minutes until the turkey is cooked through. Remove from the heat and stir in the apricots. Set aside to cool; then, taste, stir in the cilantro, and season.

4. To cook the pie, preheat the oven to 400°F (200°C, 180°C fan oven). Lay a sheet of baking parchment inside the pastry case and fill with baking beans or raw pulses or rice. Bake for 10 minutes and then carefully remove the beans and parchment. Put the pie dish on a baking tray.

5. Spoon the turkey mixture into the pastry case. Roll out the remaining pastry as described above to fit just inside the rim of the pie dish and place on top of the filling. Make a hole in the center and brush with egg.

6. Bake in the oven for about 35 minutes until golden and firm. Best served warm, straight from the dish with crisp salad.

Ingredients

gram flour to dust
1 quantity gluten free pastry, made with half gram flour and half brown rice flour
2 Tbsp. vegetable oil
1 onion, peeled and chopped
2 garlic cloves, peeled and crushed
2 Tbsp. mild curry paste
1¼ cups (300 g) skinless, boneless turkey meat, chopped
1 14-oz (400 g) can chopped tomatoes
5 Tbsp. (75 g) dried apricots, chopped
4 Tbsp. freshly chopped cilantro (coriander)
salt and freshly ground black pepper
baking beans, lentils, or rice
1 egg, beaten to glaze

DUCK AND ORANGE FILO BITES

Makes: 12   Preparation: 35 minutes plus cooling   Cooking: 15 minutes

Ingredients

3 large sheets of filo
   pastry
5 Tbsp. (75 g) butter,
   melted
7 Tbsp. (100 g) duck pâté
9 Tbsp. 125 g) cooked
   duck meat, chopped
¾ inch (2 cm) piece root
   ginger, peeled and
   finely chopped
4 tsp. dark soy sauce
9 Tbsp. (125 g) marmalade
1 Tbsp. freshly chopped
   chives
fine strips of orange zest
   to garnish

Paper thin filo pastry is the ideal choice to wrap around savory or sweet fillings. Best served warm while the pastry is crisp and buttery.

1. Line a large baking tray with baking parchment. Lay the sheets of filo on top of each other on the work surface in front of you and cut into 12 squarish pieces. Cover with damp kitchen paper.

2. Taking one square at a time, brush with butter and then lay another square on top at a slightly different angle. Brush again and repeat with one more square to make a 6-pointed star shape. Keep covered while preparing the remaining squares to make 12 pastry stars.

3. Brush each star with butter. Divide the pâté, duck meat, and ginger between the pastries and form into a mound in the center.

4. Working on one at a time, bring up all the corners around the filling, scrunching the pastry together round the filling to make a tightly scrunched but open bundle. Place on the baking tray lined with baking parchment. Once you have finished all 12, you can either cover and chill them for up to 24 hours or cook them straight away.

5. To bake, preheat the oven to 400°F (200°C, 180°C fan oven). Drizzle each with a little soy sauce and top with a small spoonful of marmalade. Brush the pastries with any remaining butter and bake for about 15 minutes until crisp and golden. Sprinkle with chopped chives and orange zest. Best served warm.

TIP: You can freeze these pastries, uncooked. Follow the recipe to the end of step 4 and then pack side by side in a rigid freezerproof container and seal. Label and freeze for up to 3 months. Cook from frozen, as above, but allow an extra 5–10 minutes to ensure they are thoroughly heated.

FISH

SMOKED FISH, RICE, AND PEA HANDFULS

Makes: 4   Preparation: 40 minutes plus chilling and cooling   Cooking: 45 minutes

Ingredients

gluten-free flour to dust
1 quantity gluten-free
   shortcrust pastry or
   standard shortcrust
   pastry
baking beans, lentils,
   or rice
1 cup 2 Tbsp. (250 g)
   smoked haddock fillet
1 bay leaf
1 Tbsp. mild curry paste
3 eggs
½ cup (150 ml) whole milk
salt and freshly ground
   black pepper
4 Tbsp. freshly chopped
   cilantro (coriander)
7 Tbsp. (100 g) cooked
   basmati rice
7 Tbsp. (100 g)
   cooked peas

My inspiration for these comes from my love of kedgeree.

1. Preheat the oven to 400°F (200°C, 180°C fan oven). Dust the work surface lightly with gluten-free flour, setting aside one third of the pastry for the fishy lids. Divide remaining pastry into four and roll out to fit four 4-inch (10-cm) round, rimless, nonstick pie dishes, approximately 1¼ inch (3 cm) deep.

2. Transfer the pastry to the dishes and press together any cracks—the pastry is quite crumbly to work with. Trim to neaten the edges and mix the trimmings into the reserved pastry. Chill the reserved pastry until required and the lined tins for at least 30 minutes.

3. Line the pastry with circles of baking parchment and fill with baking beans or lentils or rice. Put the dishes on a baking tray and bake for 10 minutes. Carefully remove the beans or rice and discard the parchment. Prick the bases all over with a fork and return to the oven for 5 minutes to "set" the pastry. Leave to cool.

4. Meanwhile, put the haddock in a frying pan with a lid, add the bay leaf, and just cover with water. Bring to a boil, cover, and simmer very gently for 5 minutes only. Leave to cool in the liquid; then, drain, flake the fish, and discard the skin and bay leaf.

5. Put the curry paste in a bowl and whisk in 2 eggs, the milk, and seasoning until well blended. Stir in the cilantro, rice, peas, and cooked fish.

6. To bake, reduce the oven temperature to 375°F (190°C, 170°C fan oven). Roll out the reserved pastry thinly and, using a 3¾-inch (9-cm) long fish-shaped cutter or template, stamp out 12 fish shapes, rerolling as necessary.

7. Divide the fish filling between the pastry cases. Arrange pastry fish on top and brush with egg. Bake in the oven for about 30 minutes until set. Stand for 10 minutes before removing from dishes. Delicious served warm or cold.

SMOKY SALMON TURNOVER

Serves: 4   Preparation: 30 minutes   Cooking: 50 minutes

I'd never come across hot smoked salmon until I moved to Scotland. Now, it is widely available, and is succulent and delicious hot or cold. You can use standard smoked salmon if unavailable or cooked smoked haddock, or mackerel or cooked prawns are good too.

1. First, make a sauce. Melt the butter in a saucepan, add the flour, and cook for 1 minute. Remove from the heat and gradually stir in the milk. Return to the heat and cook, stirring, until it reaches boiling point and then simmer for 2 minutes. Remove from the heat, stir in the spring onions, and set aside to cool; then, stir in the salmon and plenty of seasoning.

2. Preheat the oven to 375°F (190°C, 170°C fan oven). Line a baking tray with baking parchment. Make up the suet crust pastry and roll out on a lightly floured surface to make a 12-inch (30-cm) diameter circle.

3. Spoon the fish and onion mixture on one half, leaving a border of about ¾ inch (2 cm). Brush the border with beaten egg and carefully fold over the other half. Press lightly to seal the edge and then crimp the edge and transfer to the lined baking tray. Using a sharp knife, lightly slash the top.

4. Brush all over with beaten egg and bake for 40–45 minutes until golden brown and piping hot. Best served hot, sprinkled with chives, accompanied with rocket salad and lemon wedges.

Variations
Replace the salmon with smoked ham or chicken or cooked smoked bacon. For a lighter dish, leave out the cheese.

Ingredients

2 Tbsp. (25 g) butter
2 Tbsp. (25 g) flour
1 cup (300 ml) whole milk
1 bunch spring onions (scallions), trimmed and chopped
1½ cups (350 g) hot smoked salmon, skinned and flaked
salt and freshly ground black pepper
1 quantity suet crust pastry, made with vegetable suet and ¼ cup (50 g) freshly grated Parmesan cheese and 4 Tbsp. freshly chopped chives added
1 egg, beaten, to glaze
chopped chives to garnish

SALMON, SPINACH, AND WILD RICE SPELT BAKE

Serves: 6   Preparation: 40 minutes plus cooling   Cooking: 55 minutes

Ingredients

1 quantity shortcrust
  pastry, made using
  whole wheat spelt flour
baking beans, lentils, or
  rice
1 cup (225 g) baby spinach
  leaves, trimmed
7 Tbsp. (100 g) rocket
1 large leek, trimmed,
  rinsed, and finely sliced
1 cup 2 Tbsp. (200 ml)
  heavy cream
¼ tsp. grated nutmeg
salt and freshly ground
  black pepper
1¼ cups (300 g) salmon
  fillet
½ cup (115 g) cooked
  wild rice
1 egg, beaten, to glaze

Very simple flavors come together in a light, wholewheat pastry crust for this pie. Wild rice gives a slight nuttiness to the mixture, but brown rice works just as well. Use a traditional wheat flour or plain white flour shortcrust pastry if preferred.

1. Preheat the oven to 400°F (200°C, 180°C fan oven). Roll out two thirds of the pastry on a lightly floured surface to fit a 8¾-inch (22-cm) diameter rimless pie dish, 1¼ inch (3 cm) deep.

2. Transfer the pastry to the dish. Trim to neaten the edges and mix the trimmings into the remaining pastry. Chill the reserved pastry until required.

3. Line the pastry with a circle of baking parchment and fill with baking beans or lentils or rice. Put the dish on a baking tray and bake for 10 minutes. Carefully remove the beans or rice and discard the parchment. Prick the base all over with a fork and return to the oven for 5 minutes to "set" the pastry. Leave to cool.

4. Meanwhile, rinse the spinach and rocket leaves and pack into a large saucepan while still wet. Stir in the leeks, cover, and cook over a medium heat for 6–7 minutes, turning occasionally, until just wilted. Drain well through a sieve or colander, pressing the vegetables against the sides to extract as much water as possible. Leave aside to cool; then, blot with kitchen paper, put in a bowl, and mix in the cream, nutmeg, and plenty of seasoning. Set aside.

5. Put the salmon in a frying pan with a lid. Barely cover with water, bring to a boil, cover, and simmer very gently for 5 minutes only. Allow to cool in the liquid and then drain; flake the fish away from the skin and discard the skin.

6. Put the rice and salmon into the bottom of the pastry case. Top with the spinach mixture. Roll out the remaining pastry to fit the top of the pie dish.

7. Stamp out 2 small fish shapes using a cutter or template and put the pastry circle over the spinach. Press gently to seal the edges together. Brush with egg and stick the cut out pastry fishes on top to decorate. Brush with more egg and stand the pie on a baking tray. Bake for 40 minutes until lightly golden and the filling piping hot. Serve hot or cold.

SMOKED SALMON AND ASPARAGUS ENVELOPES

Makes: 4 Preparation: 30 minutes Cooking: 20 minutes

Fine asparagus works best for this recipe, but if you have the thicker stems, cut them in half lengthways. I use smoked salmon, but you can replace with wafer thin slices of Parma ham or bacon pieces or add a bit more asparagus without the fish for a vegetarian version.

1. Preheat the oven to 425°F (220°C, 200°C fan oven). Line a large baking tray with baking parchment. Roll out the pastry on a lightly floured surface to a 12-inch (30-cm) square and cut into four smaller squares.

2. Mix the soft cheese with the herbs and carefully spread over each pastry square to within ¾ inch (2 cm) of the edge. Lay slices of smoked salmon diagonally across the pastry squares, corner to corner.

3. Trim the asparagus to 7-inch (18-cm) lengths. Divide into 4 bundles of 6 and lay on the pastry square in a diagonal. Season with black pepper and brush the pastry edge with beaten egg.

4. Bring up two opposite sides of pastry and overlap them on top. Press together on top to seal. Transfer to the baking tray and brush the asparagus with oil. Brush the pastry with egg and bake in the oven for about 20 minutes until golden and tender. Best served warm.

Ingredients

½ quantity flaky pastry,
4 Tbsp. soft cheese
2 Tbsp. freshly
    chopped dill
2 Tbsp. freshly chopped
    chives
14 Tbsp. (200 g) thinly
    sliced smoked salmon
24 fine asparagus spears
Freshly ground black
    pepper
1 tsp. olive oil
1 egg, beaten, to glaze

VOL AU VENTS FRUITS DE MERE

Makes: 4   Preparation: 25 minutes   Cooking: 25 minutes

Ingredients

1 quantity puff pastry
1 egg, beaten, to glaze
2 Tbsp. extra virgin
   olive oil
4 Tbsp. olive oil
2 Tbsp. lemon juice
2 Tbsp. capers in brine,
   rinsed
1 tsp. superfine (castor)
   sugar
1½ cup (350 g) assorted
   cooked and prepared
   shellfish
4 tsp. freshly chopped dill
salt and freshly ground
   black pepper
4 Tbsp. mayonnaise
fresh dill to garnish

These impressive pastries definitely have the "wow" factor and are well worth taking time over and the extra effort of making your own puff pastry. Shellfish makes the perfect filling for buttery, flaky pastry; use all prawns or flakes of cooked salmon as an alternative if preferred.

1. Preheat the oven to 450°F (230°C, 210°C fan oven). Lightly grease a baking tray. Roll out the pastry on a lightly floured surface to form a 8-inch (20-cm) square, about ½ inch (1 cm) thick. Using a 4-inch (10-cm) plain pastry cutter, stamp out 4 rounds and place on the baking tray.

2. Cut part the way through the center of each using a 3-inch (7-cm) round cutter—this will form the lid. Brush the tops with beaten egg and bake for 20 minutes until risen and golden brown.

3. Carefully remove the inner circles of pastry and reserve as lids. Scoop out and discard the soft pastry from inside to leave crisp pastry shells. Cool the cases on a wire rack.

4. Preheat the oven to 375°F (190°C, 170°C fan oven). Put the cases on a baking tray and put back in the oven for 5 minutes until hot.

5. Meanwhile, prepare the filling. Put the oil, juice, capers, and sugar in a small saucepan and heat very gently until hot (do not boil). Put the shellfish in a heatproof bowl and toss in the dill and seasoning; then, mix in the hot dressing.

6. Spoon 1 tablespoon mayonnaise into each vol au vent case. Divide some of the warm shellfish between the cases. Sit the lids back on top, garnish, and serve immediately with the remaining shellfish on the side.

Variations

If you prefer a cold filling, simply mix the filling ingredients together and either put into cold pastry cases or reheat the cases as above. For party-sized vol au vents or bouchées, roll the pastry as above and use a 2-inch (5-cm) pastry cutter and cut out 16 rounds. Make the lid using a 1-inch (2½-cm) cutter. Bake for about 15 minutes and then fill with a finely chopped combination of your favorite ingredients.

MUSSEL, COCKLE, AND BACON POT PIES

Makes: 4   Preparation: 25 minutes plus cooling   Cooking: 30 minutes

Ingredients

¼ Tbsp. (15 g) butter
4 rindless pieces smoked streaky bacon, finely chopped
2 garlic cloves, crushed
1 small onion, finely chopped
½ cup (150 ml) dry white wine
½ cup (150 ml) fish stock
½ cup (150 ml) heavy cream
4 Tbsp. freshly chopped parsley
Salt and freshly ground black pepper
2 cups (450 g) cooked shelled mussels
14 Tbsp. (200 g) cooked cockles
½ quantity puff, flaky, or rough puff pastry
1 egg, beaten, to glaze

These pretty little pies can be made in any small round basin as long as it's ovenproof. They make generous starters or are ideal for lunch or a light supper, and don't forget the spoons for eating the creamy liquor left in the bottom!

1. Melt the butter in a small saucepan and fry the bacon, garlic, and onion for 5 minutes, stirring, until softened. Pour the wine over the mixture, bring to a boil, and simmer gently for about 5 minutes to reduce by half. Allow to cool and then stir in the stock, cream, parsley, and season to taste.

2. Wash and pat dry the mussels and cockles and then divide between 1 cup (4 x 300 ml), 4-inch (10-cm) diameter ovenproof basins or small enamel pans—use pie birds if liked. Cover and chill until required.

3. When ready to bake, preheat the oven to 425°F (220°C, 200°C fan oven). Divide the pastry into 4 equal pieces and roll out each piece on a lightly floured surface to ¾ inch (2 cm) larger all around than the basins. Make a small cross in the center of each.

4. Spoon the garlic and bacon stock over the seafood and brush the outside top edge of the basins with water. Transfer the rolled out pastry circles on top, pressing down to make a good seal over the edge of the basins.

5. Put the basins on a baking tray and brush the pastry tops with egg. Bake for about 20 minutes until risen and golden and the filling is piping hot. Serve immediately with crusty bread to mop up the juices.

Variations

If you don't like mussels, use cooked prawns or a selection of shellfish. Cooked white fish or salmon also makes a good filling.

SARDINE AND TOMATO PASTRIES

Makes: 10   Preparation: 45 minutes plus cooling   Cooking: 25 minutes

If you don't have a fish-shaped pastry cutter, make a simple shape on a piece of thick cardboard and use it as a template. These little fish look lovely "swimming" on a large platter, perfect for a buffet or cocktail party. Use canned fish if preferred.

1. Line a large baking tray with baking parchment. Preheat the grill to a medium/hot setting. Wash and pat dry the fish. Line the grill pan with foil and arrange the sardines on top, skin side down. Season and cook for about 5 minutes until cooked through. Flake the fish into a heatproof bowl. Allow to cool and then mix in the oil, garlic, tomato, parsley, and chutney.

2. Divide the pastry in half and roll out each half thinly on a lightly floured surface to 12-inch (30-cm) squares. Cut out 15½ x 2½ inch (16 x 6 cm) long fish shapes from each square. Gather up the trimmings, re-roll and cut out a further 2 fish—use these for pastry bases. You should have 20 fish in total.

3. Divide the filling between 10 fishes and evenly spread down the center of each. Brush the edges with egg. Carefully place another fish on top and press around the edge to seal. Knock up the edges.

4. If preferred, make scale patterns on the pastry using a small, sharp knife and make a small hole in each for an eye. Cover and chill until ready to bake.

5. To bake, preheat the oven to 425°F (220°C, 200°C fan oven). Remove the covering and brush the pastry fish with beaten egg. Bake in the oven for about 20 minutes until golden and puffed up. Best served warm with lemon wedges, a crisp salad, and tomato chutney.

Ingredients

14 Tbsp. (200 g) fresh sardine fillets
salt and freshly ground black pepper
1 Tbsp. olive oil
2 garlic cloves, peeled and finely chopped
1 ripe tomato, finely chopped
2 Tbsp. freshly chopped parsley
3 Tbsp. sweet tomato chutney (plus extra to serve)
1 quantity flaky pastry
1 egg, beaten to glaze

Anchovy, Olive, and Caper Mille Feuille

Makes: 6   Preparation: 30 minutes plus cooling   Cooking: 15 minutes

Ingredients

½ quantity puff pastry

1 egg, beaten

2 oz (50 g) can anchovies, drained and chopped

2 scallions (spring onions), trimmed and finely chopped

2 Tbsp. (25 g) pitted black olives, finely chopped

2 Tbsp. freshly chopped parsley

2 Tbsp. freshly chopped tarragon

2 Tbsp. freshly chopped cilantro (coriander)

2 Tbsp. capers in brine, drained and rinsed

Freshly ground black pepper

6 Tbsp. crème fraîche

These French pastries are usually made and filled with fresh cream and fruit; the name means "thousands of leaves" and refers to the flaky layers of pastry. You can make them in different sizes for serving as a starter or canapé.

1. Preheat the oven to 425°F (220°C, 200°C fan oven). Line a baking tray with baking parchment. On a lightly floured surface, roll out the pastry to make a rectangle approximately 10 x 9 inches (25 x 23 cm).

2. Carefully transfer the pastry to the tray and prick all over with a fork. Brush lightly with egg. Bake in the oven for 12–15 minutes until golden and risen. Leave to cool on the tray.

3. Carefully transfer the pastry to a board and, using a large sharp knife, cut in half lengthways and then cut each half into 6 equal slices.

4. When ready to serve, mix the remaining ingredients together except the crème fraîche. Spread 6 unglazed pastry slices with crème fraîche and sprinkle over the anchovy mixture. Top with the remaining pastry, glazed side up, and serve immediately.

Variations

For a sweet version, sprinkle the top of the pastry with 1 tablespoon superfine (castor) sugar before baking. Thinly slice 6 strawberries and lightly whip ½ cup (150 ml) heavy cream. Sandwich 2 pieces of pastry together, sugar side up, with whipped cream, sliced strawberries, and a little strawberry jam. Serve immediately.

PRAWN PIZZA PIE

Serves: 4–6   Preparation: 30 minutes plus cooling   Cooking: 35 minutes

An extra rich treat for pizza lovers. I think it was in an American diner that I first had a pizza pie, filled with meat balls and tomato sauce. This fishy version can be easily adapted to take your favorite filling. Use traditional shortcrust or gluten-free pastry if preferred.

1. Heat the oil in a saucepan and gently fry the garlic for 1–2 minutes until softened but not brown. Add the tomatoes and sugar, bring to a boil, and simmer gently for 7–8 minutes until thickened. Stir in the olives and leave to cool. Season to taste.

2. Preheat the oven to 400°F (200°C, 180°C fan oven). Roll out the pastry on a lightly floured surface to fit a 9-inch (23-cm) diameter, 1¼-inch (3-cm) deep rimless pie plate or tin. Trim to neaten the edge and then prick all over with a fork.

3. Put the plate on a baking tray and bake for about 15 minutes until lightly cooked. Set aside to cool.

4. When ready to serve, mix the prawns into the tomato sauce and spread all over the pastry case. Arrange the sliced cheese on top. Bake in the oven for about 25 minutes until lightly golden and heated through. Best served hot, sprinkled with fresh basil, whole black olives, and capers.

Variations

For a vegetarian version, leave out the prawns and replace with 1 cup (225 g) lightly cooked sliced mushrooms. Sprinkle with 2 tablespoons of freshly grated Parmesan cheese just before baking.

Ingredients

1 Tbsp. olive oil
2 garlic cloves, crushed
1 14-oz (400 g) can chopped tomatoes
1 tsp. superfine (castor) sugar
¼ cups (50 g) pitted black olives, chopped
Salt and freshly ground black pepper
½ quantity oil pastry, made with olive oil
6 Tbsp. (175 g) cooked large peeled prawns
10 Tbsp. (150 g) ball mozzarella cheese, drained and sliced
a few fresh basil leaves
2 Tbsp. (25 g) whole pitted black olives
1 Tbsp. capers in brine, drained and rinsed

TUNISIAN TUNA BRICKS

Makes: 4   Preparation: 30 minutes   Cooking: 9 minutes

Ingredients

1 6½-oz (185g) can tuna in olive oil, drained and flaked
1–2 tsp. harissa paste, see below
salt and freshly ground black pepper
1 red onion, finely sliced
1 red chili, deseeded and finely sliced, optional
4 Tbsp. freshly chopped cilantro (coriander)
4 square sheets brick or filo pastry sheets
4 eggs
vegetable oil for shallow frying
lemon wedges to serve

I wasn't sure about this Tunisian street food snack when I first came across it. But I did enjoy it very much! Brick pastry is wafer thin and very crispy. Filo pastry makes an easier-to-obtain alternative.

1. In a bowl, flake the tuna, mix with harissa paste to taste, and season. In another bowl, mix the onion, chili if using, and cilantro together and stir half into the tuna.

2. To use brick pastry, lay one sheet at a time on the work surface, shiny side down, and put one quarter of the tuna mixture in a rectangular mound in the center of the pastry. Make a slight indent in the center. Brush the pastry with water.

3. Carefully break an egg over a small bowl to drain off about half the egg white and then put the rest of the egg onto the tuna. Fold over all the sides of the pastry, pressing well to seal to end up with a folded parcel about 5 x 3½ inches (12 x 8 cm). Repeat with the remaining pastry sheets and filling. If using filo pastry, fold each sheet to make a square and follow the same instructions.

4. To cook, pour sufficient oil into a large frying pan to a depth of ½ inch (1 cm) and heat over a medium heat for about 1 minute until hot. Carefully lower 2 bricks into the oil, folded side up, and cook for 1–1½ minutes until lightly crisp and golden. Carefully turn over (the pastry is thin, so take care not to tear it) and cook for a further 2–3 minutes until richly brown and crisp. Remove from the oil with a slotted spoon, drain, and keep warm while you cook the other bricks. Serve immediately with lemon wedges, accompanied with remaining onion salad.

Harissa paste:

A fiery hot chili-based paste from North Africa, flavoured with cumin, mint, and garlic. Use a chilli paste or sauce if unavailable.

VEGETABLES

MACARONI CHEESE PIES

Makes: 6   Preparation: 40 minutes plus cooling   Cooking: 43 minutes

A favorite hearty snack hailing from Scotland. Every baker has his or her own version of these pies, and they are delicious served straight out of the oven with tomato ketchup and fries! I use pie rings to make them, but you can just as easily shape your own free-form cases.

1. Melt the butter in a saucepan and stir in the flour. Cook for 1 minute. Remove from the heat and gradually stir in the milk. Return to the heat and cook, stirring, until the mixture comes to a boil and thickens. Cook for a further 1 minute and then remove from the heat and stir in 7 tablespoons (100 g) of grated cheese. Cover the surface with a piece of greaseproof paper and set aside.

2. Meanwhile, bring a large saucepan of lightly salted water to a boil. Add the macaroni and cook for 7–8 minutes until tender. Drain well, return to the saucepan, and stir the cheese sauce into the macaroni. Season to taste, cover as above, and leave to cool.

3. Preheat the oven to 400°F (200°C, 180°C fan oven). Make up the hot water crust pastry. Roll out the pastry thinly on a lightly floured surface to enable you to cut out 4½-inch (6 x 11.5-cm) rounds using a pastry cutter. Gently press each circle into 3¾ inch (9 cm) diameter, 1½ inch (4 cm) deep pastry rings or tins. Transfer the pastry rings to a baking tray.

4. Spoon a portion of the cold macaroni cheese filling into each and pack down well, but make sure the macaroni comes to just below the pastry edge. Sprinkle with the remaining grated cheese.

5. Bake in the oven for about 35 minutes until rich golden brown. Loosen the edges with a round bladed knife and cool for 5 minutes before removing the pies. Best served hot or warm with tomato ketchup.

Ingredients

- 2 Tbsp. (25 g) butter
- 2 Tbsp. (25 g) flour
- 1 cup (300 ml) whole milk
- 14 Tbsp. (200 g) mature cheddar cheese, grated
- 10 Tbsp. (150 g) macaroni
- salt and freshly ground black pepper
- ½ quantity hot water crust pastry

A VERY VIRTUOUS VEGETABLE PIE

Serves: 4   Preparation: 30 minutes   Cooking: 48 minutes

Ingredients

2 cups (450 g) sweet potatoes, peeled and cut into small chunks

Salt and freshly ground black pepper

4 Tbsp. vegetable stock

1 cup 2 Tbsp. (250 g) zucchini (courgette), trimmed and coarsely grated

1 cup (225 g) leek, trimmed and finely shredded

2 garlic cloves, peeled and crushed

2 tsp. ground cumin

1 cup 2 Tbsp. (250 g) cooked peeled, coarsely grated beets (beetroot)

1½ cups (350 g) cooked sweetcorn kernels

4 large sheets filo pastry

1 egg, beaten, to glaze

2 tsp. cumin seeds, lightly crushed

Compared with most other pastries, filo has quite a low fat content, so if you leave out the butter and use beaten egg instead, you can enjoy a slice of comfort every now and then without feeling too guilty.

1. Put the potatoes in a saucepan, cover with water, and add a pinch of salt. Bring to a boil and cook for 7–8 minutes until tender. Drain well and then return to the saucepan and mash smoothly. Leave to cool.

2. Meanwhile, heat the stock in a frying pan until steaming and then add the zucchini, leek, garlic, and ground cumin and cook, stirring, for 3–4 minutes until slightly tender. Leave to cool.

3. When ready to assemble, preheat the oven to 400°F (200°C, 180°C fan oven). Spoon the beets into the bottom of a 12 x 7 x 1¼-inch (30 x 18 x 3-cm) baking dish. Season well and then top with sweet corn.

4. Spoon over the zucchini and leek mixture, allowing the cooking liquid to seep through the layers. Season again and then carefully spread the sweet potato mash over the top.

5. Lay the sheets of pastry on the work surface and brush with egg; then, scrunch up each sheet to make a loose rosette shape and arrange on top of the potato, making sure it is completely covered—pull the pastry rosettes apart again if necessary.

6. Stand the dish on a baking tray, brush with egg, and sprinkle with cumin seeds. Bake in the oven for about 40 minutes until golden and cooked through—cover with foil if pastry browns too quickly. Serve hot with a crisp salad.

MEDITERRANEAN BUTTER BEAN AND VEGETABLE PIE

Serves: 6   Preparation: 40 minutes plus cooling   Cooking: 1 hour

Most pies from eastern Mediterranean regions use filo pastry. I have combined a classic bean dish from the region with a flavored gluten-free pastry and come up with a melt-in-the-mouth pie which is tasty hot or cold.

1. Heat the oil in a saucepan and gently fry the garlic, carrot, celery, and onion with 3 teaspoons coriander and bay leaves for 10 minutes until softened but not browned.

2. Stir in the tomatoe paste and plenty of seasoning. Bring to a boil and simmer for 10 minutes. Leave to cool and then discard the bay leaves and stir in the beans and dill. Cover and chill until required.

3. To cook the pie, preheat the oven to 400°F (200°C, 180°C fan oven). Dust the work surface lightly with gluten-free flour and roll out two thirds of the pastry to fit a 9 ¾-inch (24-cm) round pie dish with rim. Transfer the pastry to the dish and press together any cracks—the pastry is quite crumbly to work with. Trim to neaten the edge.

4. Spread the bean filling all over the pastry and brush the edge with beaten egg. Roll out the remaining pastry as above and using a 2¼-inch (6-cm) crinkle-edged round pastry cutter, stamp out at least 15 rounds, rerolling as necessary.

5. Carefully place around the edge of the pie dish, overlapping on top of the pie filling. Place one in the center and make a hole in it.

6. Put the dish on a baking tray. Brush the pastry with beaten egg and sprinkle with remaining coriander. Bake in the oven for about 40 minutes until the pastry is cooked and golden and the filling hot. Serve straight from the dish while warm or allow to cool and chill before serving.

Ingredients

- 2 Tbsp. olive oil
- 2 garlic cloves, peeled and crushed
- 1 carrot, peeled and finely chopped
- 1 stick celery, trimmed and finely chopped
- 1 small onion, peeled and finely chopped
- 5 tsp. coriander, lightly crushed
- 2 bay leaves
- 2¼ cups (500g) tomato paste (creamed tomatoes or passata)
- salt and freshly ground black pepper
- 1½ cups (350g) cooked butterbeans
- 3 Tbsp. freshly chopped dill
- 1 quantity of gluten-free pastry, made with half fine cornmeal and half brown rice flour
- 1 egg, beaten, to glaze

RATATOUILLE PIE

Serves: 6   Preparation: 35 minutes plus cooling   Cooking: 1 hour 25 mins

Ingredients

4 Tbsp. olive oil

2½ tsp. coriander, lightly crushed

1 small onion, peeled and finely chopped

2 garlic cloves, peeled and finely chopped

1 each small red and yellow peppers, deseeded and finely chopped

1 medium eggplant (aubergine), trimmed and cut into cubes

1½ cups (250 ml) sieved tomatoes

1 bouquet garni—see below

Salt and freshly ground black pepper

1 medium zucchini (courgette), trimmed and finely diced

1 tsp superfine (castor) sugar

1 quantity oil pastry, made up with olive oil and 2 Tbsp. sun dried tomato paste added, less 2 Tbsp. water

One of my favorite vegetable dishes, ratatouille is a true taste of summer. Usually, the vegetables are quite chunky, but for a pie filling, it is best to cut them up a bit smaller. There is no need to salt the eggplant for this recipe.

1. Heat 3 tablespoons of oil in a large saucepan and then gently fry 1½ teaspoons of coriander, onion, garlic, and peppers for 10 minutes until softened but not browned. Add the eggplant and cook, stirring, for 1 minute and then pour in the sieved tomatoes and add the bouquet garni and seasoning. Bring to a boil, cover, and simmer gently for 10 minutes.

2. Stir in the zucchini, replace the lid, and to continue to cook for 10 minutes until tender but not too soft. Stir in the sugar and leave to cool. Discard the bouquet garni and season to taste.

3. Make up the oil pastry. Preheat the oven to 400°F (200°C, 180°C fan oven). Roll out just over half the pastry on a lightly floured surface to fit a 9-inch (23-cm) diameter, 1½ inch (3½ cm) deep pie plate or tin with rim. Trim to neaten the edge and spread with the ratatouille filling. Brush the edge with water.

4. Roll out the remaining pastry as above to fit the top of the pie plate and lay on top. Press the edges together to seal and make a hole in the center. Put the plate on a baking tray, brush with remaining oil, and sprinkle with remaining cilantro seeds. Bake for 45–50 minutes until lightly golden and piping hot. Serve hot or cold.

Bouquet garni:

A selection of aromatic herbs used to flavor stocks, soups, and casseroles. They are tied together in a bundle with string and are easily discarded before serving. Make your own from 2–3 sprigs of parsley, a sprig of thyme, rosemary, a bay leaf, and a celery leaf.

FILO INDIAN SAMOSAS

Makes: 12   Preparation: 30 minutes plus cooling   Cooking: 36 minutes

Usually, these tasty Indian snacks are made with a dough-like pastry, but filo makes a convenient casing which cooks to a crisp. Chop the vegetables quite small (or grate if you prefer) so that they cook quickly and fit neatly into the triangular samosa shape.

1. Put the spice seeds in a small frying pan and place over medium heat. Stir for 3–4 minutes until lightly toasted. Cool slightly and then lightly crush.

2. Meanwhile, melt the ghee or butter in a frying pan until bubbling and then gently fry the garlic, ginger, onion, crushed seeds, and finely chopped vegetables. Cook, stirring for about 20 minutes, until tender. Leave the mixture to cool and then stir in the onion seeds, cilantro, and plenty of seasoning.

3. Cut each sheet of filo into 3 long strips. Working on one strip at a time, center about 2 tablespoons (25 g) of the vegetables at one end.

4. Fold the end of the pastry strip over to make a triangular turnover shape. Keep folding over until you reach the end of the strip; then, brush the end with water and fold again to seal and form a multi-layered triangle. Continue filling and folding until you have made 12 samosas. Cover and chill until required.

5. To cook, heat the oil for deep frying to 375°F (190°C) and fry the samosas in 3 batches for 3–4 minutes, turning halfway through, until crisp and golden. Drain well and serve hot.

Ingredients

1 tsp. each mustard seeds, cumin seeds, and coriander
2 Tbsp. (25 g) ghee or butter
1 garlic clove, peeled and crushed
¾ inch (2 cm) piece root ginger, peeled and grated
1 medium onion, peeled and finely chopped
¾ cup (175 g) carrot, peeled and finely chopped
¾ cup (175 g) potato, peeled and finely chopped
1 tsp. black onion seeds
2 Tbsp. freshly chopped cilantro (coriander)
salt and freshly ground black pepper
4 large sheets of filo pastry
vegetable oil for deep frying

Variations

You can oven bake these samosas if preferred. You need to melt another ¼ cup (50 g) ghee or butter and use to brush the pastry strips as you fold them up. Place on a baking tray lined with baking parchment, brush with remaining melted ghee or butter, and bake in a preheated oven at 375°F (190°C, 170°C fan oven) for about 20 minutes.

BLUE CHEESE, CELERY, AND PEAR CROSTATA

Serves: 4   Preparation: 20 minutes   Cooking: 30 minutes

Ingredients

1 quantity double cheese pastry

2 small sweet, ripe pears, cored

2 sticks celery, trimmed and thinly sliced

½ cup (115 g) blue cheese, crumbled

2 Tbsp. (25 g) walnut pieces

1 egg, beaten, to glaze

celery leaves to garnish

A crostata is an Italian pie which is formed simply on a baking tray and has a folded edge to hold in the filling. It's the perfect solution for using very short pastry or if you don't want to go to the extra bother of using a tin.

1. Preheat the oven to 400°F (200°C, 180°C fan oven). Line the work surface with a large sheet of baking parchment and dust lightly with flour. Roll out the pastry in a round to approximately 11 inches (28 cm) diameter. Carefully slide the pastry on the parchment onto a large baking tray. Cut down the parchment to fit the baking tray.

2. Slice the pears thinly and arrange all over the pastry to within 2 inch (5 cm) of the edge. Sprinkle with celery, blue cheese, and walnut pieces.

3. Carefully fold in the pastry edge, pleating it as you go, to partially cover some of the filling. Press the pastry edge lightly to keep in place.

4. Brush the pastry with egg and bake for about 30 minutes until the pastry is golden and crisp. Best served warm, garnished with celery leaves.

Variations

These pastries look rustic yet stunning and can be varied using different pastries and fillings. They work best with fillings that require little cooking and are firm in texture. Bring out the changes by using sliced apple, fresh fig, or even halved seedless grapes instead of pear.

FLAKY BABY TOMATO PIE

Serves: 2–3   Preparation: 20 minutes   Cooking: 20 minutes

A colorful creation that will get your taste buds tingling. Simple to prepare, yet guaranteed to impress—everyone will think you've spent hours in the kitchen putting this one together! Yellow tomatoes look stunning when available, but all red works just as well.

1. Preheat the oven to 425°F (220°C, 200°C fan oven). Line a large baking tray with baking parchment. Roll out the pastry on a lightly floured surface to a rectangle 10½ x 7 inches (27 x 18 cm). Score the pastry ½ inch (1 cm) all around the edge and then score the edge diagonally with a knife. Brush the edge with egg.

2. Mix the garlic and rosemary into the pesto and spread over the inner area of pastry. Arrange the tomatoes, side by side, alternate side up, on top in a single layer.

3. Drizzle with balsamic, sprinkle with sugar, and season well. Sprinkle with a few rosemary sprigs and bake in the oven for about 20 minutes until crisp and golden and the tomatoes are just tender. Discard the cooked rosemary.

4. To serve, carefully transfer the tart to a serving platter or board. Sprinkle over the crumbled cheese, garnish with extra fresh rosemary sprigs, and serve immediately.

Variations
For a simplified version, spread the pastry case with regular green pesto. Top with the tomatoes and drizzle with olive oil before baking. Serve with shavings of fresh Parmesan cheese scattered over the top.

Ingredients

½ quantity flaky pastry,
1 egg, beaten, to glaze
2 garlic clove, peeled and crushed
1 Tbsp. freshly chopped rosemary or 1 tsp. dried
4 Tbsp. red pesto sauce
1 cup 3 Tbsp. (275 g) assorted baby plum tomatoes, halved
dash of balsamic vinegar
1 tsp. superfine (castor) sugar
salt and freshly ground black pepper
a few small sprigs fresh rosemary
¼ cup (50g) firm goat's cheese, crumbled

SPANIKOPITA

Makes: 9 Slices   Preparation: 40 minutes plus cooling   Cooking: 1 hour 15 minutes

Ingredients

4 Tbsp. olive oil
1 medium onion, peeled and chopped
1 bunch scallions (spring onions), trimmed and white and green parts chopped
2¼ cups (500 g) spinach, trimmed and shredded
a small bunch fresh dill, chopped, or 4 tsp. dried dill
a small bunch fresh continental (flat leaf) parsley, chopped
14 Tbsp. (200 g) feta cheese, finely crumbled
3 eggs, beaten
freshly ground black pepper
5 Tbsp. (75 g) butter, melted
12 large sheets filo pastry

In Greece, this pie is made during the Lenten fast and contains no cheese, eggs, or milk. This is the version many of us are more familiar with, and it is best eaten on the same day as baking.

1. Heat the oil in a large saucepan and cook the onion and scallions for 5 minutes, stirring occasionally, until softened but not browned. Add half of the spinach, mix well, cover with a lid, reduce the heat, and cook gently for 5 mins, stirring occasionally, until wilted down. Transfer to a heatproof plate.

2. Pack the remaining spinach in the same saucepan and add 2 tablespoons of water. Cover and cook for 5 minutes, stirring occasionally, until wilted down. Mix in the oniony spinach mixture to the saucepan, and cook, stirring, for a further 5 minutes; then, drain well through a sieve or colander, pressing the vegetables against the sides to extract as much water as possible. Leave to cool and then blot with kitchen paper and put in a bowl. Stir in the feta cheese, beaten eggs, and plenty of black pepper and mix well.

3. Preheat the oven to 325°F (170°C, 150°C fan oven). Grease and line a 10 x 6 ¾ x 1¼-inch (25 x 17.5 x 3-cm) cake pan with baking parchment and then brush with butter.

4. Brush a sheet of filo with butter and use to line the pan, folding it and carefully pressing it into the sides and corners of the tin so that the pastry fits snugly with a little overhanging the edges. Brush all over with butter and lay another sheet on top, folding it and pressing it down as before. Continue the buttering, layering, and pressing process until you have used 6 sheets.

5. Spread the spinach mixture into the pastry case, packing it evenly into the corners. Brush a sheet of filo with butter and fold to fit the top of the pan. Lay directly on the spinach and fold over the overlapping edges.

6. Repeat this process, using up the remaining sheets. Brush the top with any remaining butter and bake in the center of the oven for 1 hour or until the pastry is crisp and golden brown all over. Cut into 9 wedges and serve hot or slightly warm.

MINI BEANY EMPANADAS

Makes: 9   Preparation: 35 minutes plus cooling   Cooking: 13 minutes

These Mexican-style snacks are more typically made with tortilla dough as a casing, but rough puff pastry makes a good alternative and gives a wonderfully soft, flaky case; perfect for bite-sized party snacks.

1. Heat the oil in a frying pan and gently fry the garlic, chili to taste, and scallions for 2–3 minutes until softened. Set aside to cool.

2. Put the beans in a bowl and mix in the sweet corn, cilantro, and chili onion mixture. Season well.

3. Roll out the pastry on a lightly floured surface to form a 11-inch (27-cm) square. Using a 3¾-inch (9-cm) round cutter, stamp out 9 rounds of pastry. Divide the filling between the center of each. Brush the edge with water and bring up the edges, pressing them together to seal well. Place on a board lined with baking parchment, cover, and chill until required.

4. Heat about ¾ inch (2 cm) oil in a large deep frying pan until hot. Cook the empanadas over a medium heat for 4–5 minutes on each side until golden. Drain well and serve warm. Delicious accompanied with a chopped salad of avocado, tomato, and fresh cilantro with a squeeze of lime.

Variations

If preferred, you can bake these pastries. Place on a large baking tray lined with baking parchment and bake in a preheated oven at 425°F (220°C, 200°C fan oven) for about 15 minutes until crisp and golden.

Ingredients

2 tsp. olive oil
2 garlic cloves
½–1 tsp. dried chili flakes
4 scallions (spring onions), trimmed and chopped
½ cup (115 g) cooked kidney beans, mashed
½ cup (115 g) cooked sweetcorn
2 Tbsp. freshly chopped cilantro (coriander)
salt and freshly ground black pepper
½ quantity rough puff pastry
vegetable oil for shallow frying

AFTERNOON TEA EGG AND CRESS HANDFULS

Makes: 8   Preparation: 20 minutes plus cooling   Cooking: 20 minutes

Ingredients

½ quantity flaky pastry
baking beans, lentils,
    or rice
1 egg, beaten
4 hard boiled eggs,
    peeled
4 Tbsp. mayonnaise
½ tsp. English mustard,
    optional
salt and freshly ground
    black pepper
1 box/carton baby
    watercress or mustard
    and cress, rinsed and
    trimmed

I've made several versions of these pastries and settled on this one as my favorite. You can make up the cases 2 or 3 days in advance of serving and of course use them with any savory or sweet filling you may prefer.

1. Preheat the oven to 425°F (220°C, 200°C fan oven). Lightly grease a 2¾-inch (8 x 7-cm) diameter, 1¼ inch (3½ cm) deep muffin tins. Roll the pastry thinly on a lightly floured surface to make a rectangle 16 x 8 inches (40 x 20 cm). Cut into 8 squares.

2. Press each square gently into a muffin tin and line each with a small square of baking parchment. Half fill with baking beans or raw lentils or rice.

3. Bake in the oven for 10 minutes to set the pastry. Carefully remove the beans or rice and the paper. Prick the bases, brush with egg, and cook for a further 8–10 minutes until golden and cooked through. Transfer to a wire rack to cool.

4. For the filling, mash the hardboiled eggs and mix with the mayonnaise, mustard if using, and seasoning to taste. Stir in half the watercress or mustard and cress.

5. To serve, spoon the egg mixture into each pastry case. Sprinkle with the remaining cress and dust with black pepper to serve.

Variations

For a more contemporary twist, replace the cress with small leaves of wild rocket.

CREAMY ROAST GARLIC MUSHROOM PIE

Serves: 3-4   Preparation: 25 minutes plus cooling   Cooking: 45 minutes

Meaty, nutty flavored mushrooms like Portabella make the best pie fillings; they are both fleshy and tasty. They are robust enough to stand reheating. If these are unavailable, use field or flat mushrooms, but peel first.

1. Preheat the oven to 400°F (200°C, 180°C fan oven). Drizzle a shallow sided roasting tray with 1 tablespoon of oil and arrange the mushrooms on top. Mix the remaining oil with the garlic and spoon over the mushrooms. Season generously. Sprinkle with a few thyme sprigs and bake in the oven for 15 minutes until tender. Leave to cool. Discard the thyme.

2. Drain the mushrooms, reserving any pan juices, and slice thickly. Put the mushrooms and cheese in a 6 x 5 ¾ x 2-inch (18 x 14 x 5-cm) pie dish with a wide rim. Mix the reserved baking juices with the white wine and cream and pour over the mushrooms. Season to taste.

3. To make up the pie, roll out the pastry quite thickly on a lightly floured surface to just larger than the pie dish. Carefully cut some of the excess pastry into thin strips, flatten slightly, and secure onto the edge of the pie dish with water. Brush with egg.

4. Transfer the rolled out pastry to the top and press down onto the edge to seal. Make a hole in the center and brush all over with egg. Sprinkle with a few more sprigs of thyme.

5. Put the dish on a baking tray and bake for about 30 minutes until risen and golden. Serve immediately sprinkled with fresh thyme if preferred.

Ingredients

3 Tbsp. olive oil
2¼ cups (500 g) Portabella (large) mushrooms, wiped
2 garlic cloves, peeled and finely chopped
salt and freshly ground black pepper
a small bunch fresh thyme
14 Tbsp. (200 g) Gorgonzola cheese, cubed
¼ cup (50 ml) dry white wine
¼ cup (50 ml) heavy cream
¾ quantity suet crust pastry, made with vegetable suet, and 1 Tbsp. freshly chopped thyme or 1 tsp. dried thyme added
1 egg, beaten, to glaze

Variations
For a richer pie, cover with ½ quantity flaky or rough puff pastry.

FREE-FORM BEAN AND PEA PIES

Serves: 6   Preparation: 25 minutes plus cooling   Cooking: 24 minutes

Ingredients

10 Tbsp. (150 g)
    shelled peas
10 Tbsp. (150 g) shelled
    fava (broad) beans
1 quantity soft cheese
    pastry
1½ tsp. ground cumin
6 scallions (spring onions),
    trimmed and white
    and green parts finely
    chopped
2 eggs beaten
½ cup (150 ml) double
    cream
Salt and freshly ground
    black pepper

I first discovered a variation of this pastry when I was researching recipes for a Cuban cookbook. Cream cheese makes a short and slightly flaky pastry, which is an absolute joy to eat with fresh sweet spring vegetables.

1. Preheat the oven to 425°F (220°C, 200°C fan oven). Line a large baking tray with baking parchment. Bring a saucepan of water to a boil and blanch the peas and beans for 4 minutes. Drain well and rinse in cold water. Set aside in cold water.

2. Divide the pastry into 6. On a lightly floured surface, gently roll out into 6 roughly shaped 8-inch (20-cm) circles. Drain the peas and beans well and pat dry with absorbent kitchen paper. Put in a bowl and mix in the cumin and all but 2 tablespoons of scallions.

3. Carefully pile onto the center of each pastry circle and brush the edges with a little of the egg. Bring up the sides of the pastry, pleating and pinching together to enclose the vegetables and make a case, but leaving the top open—make sure you seal the sides well to avoid the filling leaking during cooking..

4. Beat 2 eggs together with the cream and plenty of seasoning and pour into each pie. Bake for about 20 minutes until golden. Sprinkle with remaining scallions and serve hot or cold with wholegrain mustard.

Variation:

You can follow the same basic recipe used above but substitute the peas and beans with blueberries and raspberries to make dessert pies. Mix 2 or 3 tablespoons of superfine (castor) sugar and 1 teaspoon vanilla extract into the egg and cream mixture and then bake as above.

WHITE NUT AND PESTO FILO PIES

Serves: 8   Preparation: 40 minutes plus cooling   Cooking: 28 minutes

These creations are perfect for an alternative Christmas dinner, and homemade pesto really makes a difference in flavor for the baked pies.

Ingredients

10 Tbsp. (150 g) butter or margarine
1 onion, peeled and finely chopped
1 cup 2 Tbsp. (250 g) assorted unsalted almonds, pine nuts, and cashews, chopped
5 Tbsp. (75 g) fresh white breadcrumbs
salt and freshly ground black pepper
pinch of ground mace or nutmeg
1 egg, beaten
8 large sheets filo pastry
1 quantity fresh pesto sauce—see below

1. Melt ¼ cup (50 g) butter or margarine in a frying pan and gently fry the onion for 7–8 minutes until softened but not browned. Let cool for 20 minutes.

2. Put the nuts in a bowl and stir in the breadcrumbs along with plenty of seasoning, spice, and the onion mixture. Add the egg and mix well to form a stiff stuffing mixture. Set aside.

3. Preheat the oven to 400°F (200°C). Line 2 large baking trays with baking parchment. Melt the remaining butter or margarine. Working on one sheet of pastry at a time, brush with melted fat, fold in half, and brush again.

4. Spoon ⅛ of the nut filling on one side of the pastry to within ¾ inch (2 cm) of the edges; flatten slightly, and spoon ⅛ of the pesto on top. Fold the edges over the nut filling and brush the edges with butter.

5. Keep folding the pastry over until you have an envelope-shaped parcel. Press the edges together to seal and transfer to a baking tray.

6. Continue the pie making to use up all the pastry and filling. Brush with remaining butter, make a slit in the top of each, and bake in the oven for about 20 minutes until golden and crisp. Best served warm.

Homemade pesto (makes 3½ Tbsp. or 200 g)

Put 1 peeled garlic clove in a blender or food processor with ½ tablespoon (15 g) fresh basil, 5 tablespoons (75 g) pine nuts, ¼ cup (50 g) finely grated fresh Parmesan cheese, and 4 tablespoons of extra virgin olive oil. Season well and blend until smooth. Store in a sealed jar in the refrigerator for up to 10 days.

GOLDEN VEGETABLE PASTIES

Serves: 8   Preparation: 30 minutes plus cooling Cooking: 33 minutes

Mustard goes very well with sweet vegetables, and the natural sweetness is enhanced by grated apple. For extra zing, mix in some finely grated orange zest.

1. Put the carrots and ginger in a saucepan; cover with water and bring to a boil. Cook for 7–8 minutes. Drain well, return to the saucepan, and mash with a fork. Leave to cool.

2. Meanwhile, bring a small saucepan of water to a boil and cook the baby corn for 4–5 minutes until tender. Drain well, leave to cool, and then mix into the carrot.

3. Peel, core, and grate the apple. Mix into the cooked vegetables along with the mustard and plenty of seasoning.

4. Preheat the oven to 425°F (220°C, 200°C fan oven). Line a large baking tray with baking parchment. Divide the pastry in 2 and roll out each half on a lightly floured surface to form a 12-inch (30-cm) square. Using a 6-inch (15-cm) saucer or round cutter, stamp out 4 rounds of pastry from each.

5. Divide the filling between the center of each pastry round. Brush the edge with water and fold in half; press the edges together and carefully crimp the edges between your thumb and forefinger.

6. Transfer to the baking tray, brush with the egg, and sprinkle lightly with mustard seeds. Bake in the oven for about 20 minutes until golden and puffy. Best served warm.

Ingredients

10 Tbsp. (300 g) carrots, peeled and chopped
1 inch (2½ cm) root ginger, peeled and finely chopped
10 Tbsp. (150 g) baby corn, trimmed and sliced
1 eating apple
2 Tbsp. whole grain mustard
salt and freshly ground black pepper
1 quantity wholewheat rough puff pastry,
1 egg, beaten
1 Tbsp. mustard seeds, lightly crushed

Variations

Try parsnip, turnip, or rutabaga (swede) instead of carrot; you can also use the flesh of butternut squash. Adjust the initial boiling period accordingly to make sure the root vegetable cooks properly.

EAST MEETS WEST

Serves: 4   Preparation: 30 minutes plus cooling   Cooking: 34 minutes

Some vegetables are too delicate for conventional pie cooking. For this recipe, the pastry part gets cooked first and then is filled with "just cooked" Asian vegetables and topped with a crisp crumb to finish.

1. Preheat the oven to 400°F (200°C, 180°C fan oven). Roll out the pastry on a lightly floured surface to fit a 9inch (18cm) diameter, 1¾inch (4cm) deep pie tin with a rim. Trim to neaten the edge and then press the edge with a fork.

2. Place a circle of baking parchment in the center. Fill with baking beans or raw lentils or rice. Stand the tin on a baking tray and bake for 10 minutes. Carefully remove the beans or rice and paper. Prick the base all over with a fork and return to the oven for a further 8–10 minutes until the pastry is lightly golden and cooked through. Set aside, in the tin, on a wire rack. If preferred, when cold, slip the pastry case out of the tin.

3. Meanwhile, heat 2 tablespoons of oil in a frying pan until bubbling and stir fry the breadcrumbs for 5 minutes until crisp and lightly golden. Remove from the heat and stir in the sesame seeds and chives and keep warm.

4. Heat the remaining oil in a wok or large frying pan and stir fry the garlic, chili, scallions, broccoli, and baby corn for 2–3 minutes. Add the pak choi and continue to stir fry for a further 2–3 minutes. Add the sauce and stir fry for a further 2–3 minutes until just tender.

5. Spoon the vegetables into the pastry case using a slotted spoon. Sprinkle the crumbs on top and serve immediately.

Tip: Once assembled, you can keep this pie on a low heat (about 300°F, 150°C, 130°C fan oven) for up to 20 minutes until you are ready to serve.

Ingredients

½ quantity shortcrust pastry, with 3 Tbsp. toasted sesame seeds added
Baking beans, raw lentils, or rice
3 Tbsp. vegetable oil
¼ cup (50 g) fresh white breadcrumbs
2 Tbsp. toasted sesame seeds
2 Tbsp. freshly chopped chives
2 garlic cloves, peeled and chopped
1 red chili, deseeded and thinly sliced
4 scallions (spring onions), trimmed and chopped
7 Tbsp. (100 g) very small sprouting broccoli, trimmed
7 Tbsp. (100 g) baby corn, trimmed and sliced lengthwise
7 Tbsp. (100 g) baby pak choi leaves, trimmed
3 Tbsp. oyster sauce or 1 Tbsp. dark soy sauce plus 2 Tbsp. sweet chili sauce

SWEET

FRENCH-STYLE CUSTARD PIES

Serves: 8   Preparation: 40 minutes plus cooling   Cooking: 30 minutes

Ingredients

3 large egg yolks
½ cup (115 g) superfine (castor) sugar
3 Tbsp. flour
1 tsp. good quality vanilla extract
1 cup (300 ml) whole milk
1 quantity pâté sucrée
1 egg, beaten, to glaze
1 Tbsp. confectioner's (icing) sugar

Certainly too good for circus clowns, I discovered this rich dessert looking through a French cookbook. It comes from the Basque region, and is a thick custard tart referred to as a cake. These mini versions are rich and decadent. Perfect served with fresh soft fruit or poached pears.

1. Grease 2¾ inch (8 x 7 cm) diameter 1½ inch (3½ cm) deep muffin tins. First, make the filling. Whisk the egg yolks together with the sugar until thick and pale. Sieve the flour and fold in using a metal spoon. Gradually whisk in the vanilla and milk. Pour into a saucepan and cook over low heat, stirring, until quite thick, taking care not to burn. Cover the surface with a sheet of buttered greaseproof paper and leave to cool.

2. Meanwhile, roll out ¾ of the pastry on a lightly floured surface and stamp out 4 inch (8 x 10 cm) circles to fit into the prepared tins. Gently press the pastry into each tin. Neaten the edges and chill until required.

3. Spoon cold custard in to the pastry cases to almost fill. Roll out the remaining pastry thinly and cut out 2½-inch (8 x 6-cm) rounds. Brush the inside edge of the pastry cases with beaten egg and gently press a pastry circle on top of each. Pinch the edges together to seal. Make a small hole in the center of each. Cover and chill for 30 minutes.

4. Preheat the oven to 375°F (190°C, 170°C fan oven). Brush the top of the pastry with egg and bake in the oven for about 25 minutes until golden and firm to the touch. Allow to cool for 10 minutes in the tins and then carefully run a knife around the edge of each to remove them from the tin. Transfer to a wire rack to cool. Dust with confectioner's (icing) sugar and serve cold with fruit and pouring cream.

VANILLA PRUNE PUFF

Serves: 6   Preparation: 20 minutes plus cooling   Cooking: 20 minutes

Not many ingredients are necessary to make this fruity, sweet, French-style pastry. Choose the softest, juiciest, best quality prunes you can find for this recipe; Agen prunes are particularly good if you can track them down.

1. Preheat the oven to 425°F (220°C, 200°C fan oven). Line a baking tray with baking parchment. Divide the pastry in two. On a lightly floured surface, roll out one half to make a circular shape about 9 inches (23 cm) in diameter. Carefully transfer to the lined baking tray.

2. Put the butter in a small bowl. Split the vanilla pod in half and scrape out the black seedy paste from both halves and mix into the butter. Spread the vanilla butter sparingly all over the pastry round to within ½ inch (1 cm) of the edge and sprinkle with the sugars.

3. Arrange the prunes neatly and evenly on top. Brush the edge of the pastry with water.

4. Roll out the other half of the pastry in the same way and place on top of the prunes. Press the pastry layers together to seal and knock up the edges to neaten and create a good seal.

5. Brush the top of the pastry with egg and prick lightly with a fork. Bake in the oven for about 20 minutes until richly golden brown and puffed up. Best served warm, dusted with confectioner's (icing) sugar, and accompanied with crème fraîche.

Ingredients

½ quantity puff pastry
2 Tbsp. (25 g) unsalted butter, softened
1 vanilla pod
2 Tbsp. superfine (castor) sugar
1 Tbsp. vanilla sugar
1¼ cups (300 g) soft pitted prunes
1 egg, beaten, to glaze
1 Tbsp. confectioner's (icing) sugar

DEEP DISH SWEET SPICED APPLE PIE

Serves: 8   Preparation: 40 minutes plus cooling   Cooking: 70 minutes

Ingredients

1½ quantity sweet
   shortcrust pie pastry
4 cups (900 g) cooking
   apples
Finely grated rind and
   juice of 1 large lemon
½ cup (115 g) light
   brown sugar
2 Tbsp. cornstarch
   (cornflour)
1½ tsp. ground cinnamon
¼ cup (50 g) sultanas
2 Tbsp. (25 g) unsalted
   butter
1 egg, beaten, to glaze
1 Tbsp. superfine (castor)
   sugar

A classic family dessert pie, popular with all generations. There's lots of apple in the filling in this recipe, and it's delicately flavored with spices and lemon.

1. Preheat the oven to 400°F (200°C, 180°C fan oven). Roll out ⅔ of the pastry on a lightly floured surface and use to line a 9-inch (23-cm) diameter, 1½ inch (4 cm) deep pie dish with a rim. Trim and keep the trimmings.

2. Meanwhile, peel, core, and thinly slice the apples. Place in a bowl and toss in the lemon rind and juice. In another bowl, mix the brown sugar, cornstarch, and spice together.

3. Sprinkle a little of the sugar mixture over the base of the pastry case and mix the remainder into the apples along with the sultanas. Pile half of the apple mixture into the pastry case and push in a pie bird or funnel. Pile in the remaining apple (to come above the rim of the dish) and dot the top with the butter.

4. Roll out the remaining pastry as above to fit the top of the pie, and make a cross in the center. Brush the pie edge with egg and press the pie lid on top. Trim and seal the edge. Roll out the trimmings and cut out apple and leaf shapes and secure on the pie with egg.

6. Brush the pastry top with egg and sprinkle with superfine (castor) sugar . Stand the dish on a baking tray and bake for 30 minutes to evenly brown and then reduce the oven temperature to 350°F (180°C, 160°C fan oven). Cover the pie with foil and continue to bake for a further 40 minutes until the apple is tender—push a skewer into the center to see if cooked. Serve the pie straight from the dish, hot or cold, with custard or ice cream.

BERRY FRUITFULS

Serves: 4   Preparation: 50 minutes plus chilling and cooling   Cooking: 35 minutes

1. Preheat the oven to 400°F (200°C, 180°C fan oven). Sieve the flour and salt into a bowl and rub in the butter until well blended. Stir in 5 tablespoons (75 g) of sugar and bind together with approximately 3 tablespoons of cold water to bring the mixture together. Knead lightly to form a smooth dough. Wrap and chill for 30 minutes.

2. Set aside ¼ of the pastry and then divide the remaining pastry into 4 pieces. On a lightly floured surface, roll each piece to fit a 5-inch (4 x 12-cm) diameter, 1¼ inch (3½ cm) deep rimless pie tin. Trim, cover, and chill until required.

3. For the filling, put ¾ cups 2 tablespoons (200 g) of berries in a saucepan with 1 tablespoon of water. Bring to a boil, cover, and simmer for 3–4 minutes until very soft. Cool slightly and then push through a nylon sieve to make a purée. Return to the saucepan.

4. Mix the cornstarch with 2 tablespoons of water to form a paste and add to the fruit purée along with all but 2 tablespoons of the remaining sugar. Bring to a boil, stirring, and cook until thickened. Remove from the heat and stir in the reserved berries. Leave to cool.

5. Spoon the cooled filling into the pastry cases. Roll out the remaining pastry thinly and cut out 4-inch (4 x 10-cm) round lids. Brush the inside edge of the pastry cases with egg white and push the the lids on top. Press the edges together to seal well. Place on a large baking tray. Make small holes in the center of each.

6. Roll out the trimmings to make fruit decorations. Brush the pie top with egg white, stick on the decorations if using, and dredge with remaining sugar . Bake for 30 minutes or until golden. Serve hot or cold with pouring cream.

Ingredients

1 cup 2 Tbsp. (250 g) flour
¼ tsp. salt
20 Tbsp. (150 g) unsalted
  butter
¾ cup (175 g) superfine
  (castor) sugar
1 egg white, lightly beaten
2½ cups, 2 Tbsp. (600 g)
  prepared blueberries,
  blackberries, and
  raspberries
1 Tbsp. cornstarch
  (cornflour)

COCONUT AND LIME MERINGUE PIE

Serves: 6   Preparation: 30 minutes plus cooling   Cooking: 35 minutes

Ingredients

½ quantity sweet
   shortcrust pastry
Baking beans, raw lentils,
   or rice
2 Tbsp. cornstarch
   (cornflour)
¾ cup (175 g) superfine
   (castor) sugar
Juice and finely grated
   rind of 3 limes
1 cup (300 ml) canned
   coconut milk
a few drops green food
   coloring, optional
2 medium egg whites

The rich and exotic flavors of coconut and lime give a delicious, contemporary twist to a classic lemon meringue pie.

1. Preheat the oven to 400°F (200°C, 180°C fan oven). On a lightly floured surface, roll out the pastry thinly to fit a 9-inch (23-cm) diameter, 1½ inch (3 cm) deep pie or flan tin with rim. Fit the pastry to the tin, trim, and place a circle of baking parchment in the center. Fill with baking beans or raw lentils or rice.

2. Put the tin on a baking tray and bake for 10 minutes. Carefully remove the beans or rice and paper. Prick the base all over with a fork and return to the oven for a further 8–10 minutes until the pastry is lightly golden and cooked through. Set aside, in the tin, on a wire rack. Remove the pastry case from the tin.

3. Meanwhile, mix the cornstarch, 5 tablespoons (75 g) of sugar, and lime juice together in a saucepan to form a paste. Add the coconut milk and cook over a medium heat, stirring all the time, until boiling and then simmer for 1 minute. Stir in the lime rind and add a few drops of green coloring if using. Pour into the pastry case and set aside to cool completely.

4. In a clean bowl, whisk the egg whites until very stiff and gradually whisk in the remaining sugar to make a thick, glossy meringue.

5. Pipe or spoon the meringue over the lime filling to cover completely. Put the pie on a baking tray and bake in the oven for about 10 minutes until evenly browned. Serve hot or cold.

Variation
If you prefer something more traditional, replace the lime rind and juice with the juice and rind of one large lemon and use heavy cream instead of coconut milk.

QUINCE "PASTIES"

Ingredients

1 quantity soft cheese
   pastry
1 cup 2 Tbsp.
   (250 g) quince paste
   (membrillo), cut into
   16 portions
1 egg white, lightly
   beaten, to glaze
2 Tbsp. superfine (castor)
   sugar mixed with
   1 tsp. ground
   cinnamon

A melt-in-the-mouth variation of the simple jam turnover. Use your favorite jam, pie filling, or thinly sliced fruit if you prefer. For complete decadence, use chocolate or caramel spread. Allow the pastries to cool for a few minutes before serving; the filling retains heat and may scald.

1. Line 2 baking trays with baking parchment. Lightly dust the work surface with flour. Divide the dough into 16 equal pieces. Taking one piece of dough at a time, roll it into a ball and then roll out with a rolling pin to form a 4-inch (10-cm) circle.

2. Place a portion of quince paste in the center and brush the edge lightly with water. Carefully fold the pastry over and secure the edges by pinching together. Sit fold side down on the work surface to flatten the bottom and then place on the baking tray. Repeat to make 16. Cover loosely and chill for 30 minutes.

3. Preheat the oven to 400°F (200°C, 180°C fan oven). Discard the covering, brush lightly with beaten egg white, and sprinkle lightly with cinnamon sugar. Bake for about 15 minutes until golden and crisp. Cool for 15 minutes and then serve while still warm. Delicious served hot with clotted cream.

Variation

You can use this idea to make alternative mince pies for serving at Christmas by replacing the jam with readymade mince meat. Follow the above method using regular sweet shortcrust or puff pastry if preferred.

CHERRY NICE CHOCOLATE PIE

Serves: 8   Preparation: 35 minutes plus cooling and standing   Cooking: 40 minutes

1. Make and bake pastry case below using ⅔ of the pastry. Reduce the oven temperature to 350°F (180°C, 160°C fan oven). Spread the jam over the base of the pastry case and arrange the cherry halves on top. Set aside.

2. Put the butter and chocolate in a heatproof bowl over a saucepan of gently simmering water until melted. Remove from the water and set aside. Whisk the eggs and superfine sugar together until pale and creamy.

3. Gently fold the melted chocolate and butter into the egg mixture and spoon over the pastry. Smooth the surface.

4. Roll out the remaining chocolate pastry to a roughly shaped rectangle approximately 10 inch (25 cm) long. Cut into approximately 12 thin strips, rerolling as necessary, and arrange on top of the pie to form a lattice. Secure the edges onto the edge of the pastry case using a little water.

5. Put the tin on a baking tray and bake for about 25 minutes until the top has formed a crust and the pastry is set. Stand for 10 minutes before removing from the tin to serve hot or allow to cool in the tin and chill for at least 1 hour. Delicious with vanilla or chocolate ice cream.

Chocolate pie pastry: makes 1½ cups 2 Tbsp. (375 g)

Sieve all purpose (plain) flour, cocoa, salt, and sugar into a bowl. Rub in unsalted butter to form a mixture that resembles fresh breadcrumbs. Mix in egg yolk and a few drops of vanilla extract and bring the mixture together, adding 3–4 teaspoons of whole milk if necessary. Knead gently to form a firm dough. Wrap and chill for 30 minutes. Roll out ⅔ of the pastry thinly on a lightly floured surface to fit a 9½-inch (24-cm) diameter, 1¾ inch (4 cm) deep pie tin with rim. Prick the base all over with a fork and bake in the oven at 400°F (200°C, 180°C fan oven) for about 15 minutes until set and firm to the touch. The remaining pastry can be used as a pastry lattice for the top.

Ingredients

1 quantity chocolate pie pastry see below
6 Tbsp. good quality cherry jam
14 Tbsp. (200 g) fresh cherries, pitted and halved, or canne
6 Tbsp. (85 g) unsalted butter
7 Tbsp. (100 g) dark 72% cocoa chocolate, broken into piece
2 eggs, beaten
¼ cup (50 g) superfine (castor) sugar
cocoa powder and confectioner's (icing) sugar to dust

Chocolate Pie Pastry
¾ cup (175 g) all purpose (plain) flour
1½ Tbsp. cocoa
A pinch of salt
6 Tbsp. (75 g) caster (superfine) sugar
6 Tbsp. (75 g) unsalted butter
1 egg yolk
vanilla extract
whole milk if desired

MINI LEMON ROLY POLLIES

Makes: 4   Preparation: 20 minutes   Cooking: 25 minutes

Ingredients

14 Tbsp. (200 g)
    self-rising flour
pinch of salt
7 Tbsp. (100 g)
    vegetable suet
5 Tbsp. (75 g) superfine
    (castor) sugar
Finely grated rind of
    1 unwaxed lemon
½ cup (150 ml) freshly
    squeezed lemon juice
5 Tbsp. good quality
    lemon curd
1 egg, beaten, to glaze
4 tsp. Demerara sugar
custard to serve

Roly pollies are a traditional British nursery pudding usually made with jam. Here, I combine the flavors from a sweet suet crust pudding from my childhood called Sussex Pond Pudding. This version is a bit kinder on the hips but still extremely lemony and comforting.

1. Preheat the oven to 400°F (200°C, 180°C fan oven). Line a large baking tray with baking parchment. Make up the lemon suet crust by mixing together the flour, salt, suet, sugar, and lemon rind. Add enough of the lemon juice, mixing at the same time, to make a light, elastic dough.

2. Turn dough onto a lightly floured surface and knead very gently until smooth. Divide the mixture into 4 equal pieces. Roll out each piece to make a 5 x 6½-inch (12 x 16-cm) rectangle. Spread with the lemon curd to within ½ inch (1 cm) of the edges.

3. Brush the edges with beaten egg and carefully roll up each one, starting from one of the shorter sides. Press lightly to seal the edge and place seam-side down on the baking tray.

4. Brush all over with beaten egg, sprinkle with Demerara sugar. Bake for about 25 minutes until golden brown and risen—they will probably split on baking. Best served hot or warm with lots of custard.

JUST PEACHY FILO CRISP

Serves: 4   Preparation: 25 minutes plus cooling   Cooking: 33 minutes

Ingredients

1 unwaxed lemon
1 Tbsp. cornstarch
    (cornflour)
4 Tbsp. superfine
    (castor) sugar
6 cardamom pods, split
4 ripe peaches, peeled if
    preferred—see below
4 large sheets filo pastry
1 egg, beaten, to glaze
2 tsp. confectioner's
    (icing) sugar

This pie is perfect for summer when the juiciest, sweetest peaches are around. Cardamom spice has a citrusy note and therefore combines perfectly with fresh lemon.

1. Using a vegetable peeler, pare off 3 strips of lemon rind into a small saucepan. Add the juice and blend in the cornstarch and 3 tablespoons of superfine sugar. Remove the black seeds from the cardamom pods, grind finely, and add to the saucepan.

2. Gradually blend in 14 tablespoons (200 ml) cold water. Bring to a boil, stirring, and simmer gently for 1 minute. Remove from heat; cover the top of the sauce directly with a piece of greaseproof paper, and leave to cool.

3. Preheat the oven temperature to 400°F (200°C, 180°C fan oven). Halve and slice the peaches and place in a 3-cup (900-ml) oval pie dish—or a dish approximately 8 x 6 x 1 ¾ inches (20 x 15 x 4.5 cm). Hold a sieve over the dish and strain the cold lemon sauce through onto the peaches.

4. Lay the sheets of pastry on the work surface and brush with egg; then, scrunch up each sheet to make a loose "rosette" shape and arrange on top to cover the peaches—pull the pastry rosettes apart again if necessary.

5. Brush with more egg and sprinkle with remaining sugar. Put the dish on a baking tray and bake in the oven for about 30 minutes until golden, crisp, and hot. Serve immediately, dusted with confectioner's sugar.

How to peel peaches

Prick the stalk end of a ripe peach with a fork. Place in a heatproof bowl and cover with boiling water. Leave for about 30 seconds to loosen the skin and then plunge into cold, iced water. Carefully peel away the skin. Brush with lemon juice to prevent discoloration.

BUTTERSCOTCH CREAM PIE

Serves: 6–8   Preparation: 30 minutes plus cooling and chilling   Cooking: 20 minutes

When I was at school, every now and then we would be given a dessert called butterscotch tart. I loved it. The pastry bit wasn't great, but the butterscotch custard filling was gorgeous. This is my grown-up version, and I use nicer, sweet pastry to suit my adult palate.

1. Preheat the oven to 375°F (190°C, 170°C fan oven). Roll out the pastry to fit a 9-inch (23-cm) diameter, 1½ inch (3½ cm) deep pie tin or dish with rim. Trim to neaten the edge, prick the base all over with a fork, and bake in the oven for about 15 minutes until lightly golden and crisp. Leave to cool.

2. For the filling, melt the butter in a saucepan and mix in the sugar. Stir over a low heat until dissolved. Remove from the heat. Blend the cornstarch with a little of the milk to make a paste and mix the remaining milk into the buttery sugar.

3. Stir in the cornstarch paste and return to the heat. Cook, stirring, bring to a boil, and simmer for 1 minute to make a thick custard sauce. Stir in the vanilla and salt.

4. Pour the hot custard into the pastry case and leave to cool; then, chill for 1 hour.

5. To serve, spoon dollops of crème fraîche around the edge and sprinkle with crushed butterscotch. Delicious accompanied with fresh strawberries.

Ingredients

½ quantity pâté sucrée made up with a few drops vanilla extract added

10 Tbsp. (150 g) unsalted butter

10 Tbsp. (150 g) Demerara sugar

1½ cups (350 ml) whole milk

1 Tbsp. cornstarch (cornflour)

1 tsp. good quality vanilla extract

pinch of salt

14 Tbsp. (200 g) crème fraîche

¼ cup (50 g) butterscotch, crushed

FESTIVE FRUIT AND MARZIPAN PIES

Serves: 12   Preparation: 30 minutes plus cooling   Cooking: 30 minutes

Once you've tried these, you'll never want to make a standard mince pie again. Using a hot water crust pastry case for mincemeat and marzipan means that these little pies aren't as sweet as the more traditional shortcrust pastry versions. I prefer to make the hot water crust pastry for sweet pies using white vegetable fat instead of lard.

1. Preheat the oven to 400°F (200°C, 180°C fan oven). Make up the hot water crust pastry. Roll out the pastry thinly on a lightly floured surface and cut out 3½-inch (12 x 9-cm) rounds using a round pastry cutter, rerolling as necessary. Gently press each circle into 2¾-inch (7-cm) diameter, 1¼ inch (3½ cm) deep muffin tins. Discard the trimmings.

2. In a bowl, mix together the mincemeat, grated apple, cranberries, and spice together. Spoon a portion of the fruity filling into each tin and pack down well. Stand the tins on a baking tray. Bake in the oven for about 30 minutes until rich golden brown.

3. Meanwhile, roll out the marzipan thickly and cut out 2-inch (12 x 5-cm) star shapes, rerolling as necessary. Set aside.

4. When the pies are cooked, place a star on each pie. Loosen the edges of the pies with a round-bladed knife and cool for 10 minutes before carefully removing from the tins and transferring to a wire rack. Best served warm, dusted with confectioner's sugar, and accompanied with pouring cream.

Ingredients

½ quantity hot water crust pastry, made with white vegetable fat and all-purpose (plain) flour
1¼ cup (300 g) mincemeat
10 Tbsp. (150 g) cooking apple, peeled, cored, and grated
5 Tbsp. (75 g) dried cranberries
1 tsp. ground mixed spice
7 Tbsp. (100 g) golden or natural marzipan
1 Tbsp. confectioner's (icing) sugar

PLUM AND ALMOND CROSTATA

Serves: 6–8   Preparation: 30 minutes plus cooling   Cooking: 40 minutes

Ingredients

1 quantity extra rich
  shortcrust pastry
14 Tbsp. (200 g) ground
  almonds
9 Tbsp. (125 g) superfine
  (castor) sugar
1 tsp. good quality
  almond extract
2 eggs, beaten
1½ cups (350 g) plums,
  washed, pitted, and
  thickly sliced
2 Tbsp. (25 g) unsalted
  butter
2 Tbsp. Demerara sugar

If you can find some greengages, try using them in this recipe. The almondy filling combines superbly with their fresh, fruity flavor. Otherwise, any other plum or even apricots work just as well in this free-form rustic pastry.

1. Preheat the oven to 400°F (200°C, 180°C fan oven). Line the work surface with a large sheet of baking parchment and dust lightly with flour. Roll out the pastry in a round to approximately 14½ inches (36 cm) in diameter. Trim the edge to neaten and then carefully slide the pastry on the paper onto a large baking tray. Cut down the parchment to fit the baking tray.

2. Mix together the ground almonds, sugar, and almond extract. Bind together well using one of the eggs. Press the almond paste to form a circle in the center of the pastry, approximately 2 inches (5 cm) away from the sides. Arrange the plum slices on top.

3. Carefully fold over the pastry edge, pleating it as you go, to partially cover some of the filling. Press the pastry edge lightly to keep in place. Dot the plums with butter and sprinkle with Demerara sugar.

4. Brush the pastry with egg and bake for about 40 minutes until the pastry is golden and the plums tender. Best served warm.

Variation

You can use one of the flaky pastries for this type of Italian pie too. Roll out ½ quantity flaky or puff pastry to make a 12-inch (30-cm) round. Follow the method above, but only leave 1 inch (2½ cm) clear pastry around the edge. Brush with egg and fold the pastry over itself to make a rim. Press with a fork to seal, fill, and brush with egg. Bake as above until the pastry is risen and crisp.

GOOSEBERRY AND ELDERFLOWER JALOUSIE

Serves: 4-6   Preparation: 30 minutes plus cooling   Cooking: 30 minutes

Pronounced "ja-loo-zee," this pastry dessert takes its name from the slatted effect on its lid, resembling a louvre or "jalousie" window.

1. Put the gooseberries in a saucepan with 5 tablespoons (75 g) of sugar and 2 tablespoons of water. Bring to a boil, cover, and simmer for 8–10 minutes until softened but still holding shape. Leave to cool.

2. Whisk the egg yolk and 2 tablespoons (25 g) of sugar together until pale, thick, and creamy. Whisk in the flour, cornstarch, and 2 tablespoons of milk to make a smooth paste. Heat the remaining milk to just below boiling point and then pour over the egg and flour paste, whisking until smooth and well combined.

3. Transfer to a saucepan and stir over a low heat until boiling and then cook for a further 2 minutes until thick. Cool for 10 minutes and then mix in the cordial. Cover the surface with buttered, greaseproof paper and leave to cool.

4. Preheat the oven to 425°F (220°C, 200°C fan oven). Line a large baking tray with baking parchment. Divide the pastry into two pieces. On a lightly floured surface, roll ½ of the pastry to a 11 x 6-nch (28 x 15-cm) rectangle. Carefully transfer to the baking tray.

5. Spread with cold custard, leaving a 1-inch (2½-cm) gap on both sides, and spoon over the gooseberries. Brush both edges with the egg white. Roll the other half of the pastry into a rectangle slightly bigger than the bottom. Using a sharp knife, cut approximately ¾ inch (2 cm) wide slashes in the pastry across its width, leaving a ¾-inch (2-cm) border around the edge.

6. Lay the slatted pastry on the fruit and custard so that it opens slightly. Press down gently to seal. Knock up the edges and brush with egg white. Sprinkle with remaining sugar and bake for about 20 minutes until golden. Serve warm or cold.

Ingredients

- 1¼ cup (300 g) firm green gooseberries, topped and tailed
- ½ cup (115 g) superfine (castor) sugar
- 1 egg, separated
- 1 Tbsp. flour
- 1 Tbsp. cornstarch (cornflour)
- 14 Tbsp. (200 ml) whole milk
- 2 Tbsp. elderflower cordial
- ½ quantity puff pastry

MOROCCAN SNAKE PIE (M'HANNCHA)

Serves: 6   Preparation: 40 minutes plus cooling   Cooking: 40 minutes

Ingredients

- 5 Tbsp. (75 g) shelled unsalted pistachios, very finely chopped
- 5 Tbsp. (75 g) blanched almonds, very finely chopped
- 5 Tbsp. (75 g) pitted dates, minced
- 5 Tbsp. (75 g) unsalted butter, melted
- 1 tsp. good quality almond extract
- 7 Tbsp. (100 g) + 2 tsp. confectioner's (icing) sugar
- ½ tsp. finely grated orange rind
- approximately 4 tsp. essence of pure orange blossom, optional
- 6 square sheets brick pastry or 6 large sheets filo pastry
- 1 egg, beaten, to glaze
- 1 tsp. ground cinnamon

It was a toss-up between this recipe and baklava as to which Middle Eastern-style pastry to include. In the end, I decided to give this one some exposure instead. Traditionally made with all nuts, I add dates for moistness. The name will certainly get everyone talking!

1. Put the nuts in a bowl and mix in the dates, all but 1 tablespoon of melted butter, almond extract, 7 tablespoons (100 g) of confectioner's sugar, and orange rind. Gradually add sufficient orange blossom essence to taste if using. Mix well to make a firm paste. Set aside.

2. Preheat the oven to 350°F (180°C, 160°C fan oven). Grease and line a 7-inch (18-cm) loose-bottomed cake tin and brush with remaining butter.

3. To use brick pastry, lay one sheet on the work surface shiny side down in front of you. Divide the almond filling into 6 equal pieces and spread one portion of filling toward the bottom edge of the pastry in a sausage shape along its length.

4. Roll up tightly in the pastry, brushing with water to seal and place inside the tin, pushed snugly to the edge. Repeat with the remaining sheets and filling, laying the coils in the tin, side by side, so that they fill the tin as a complete coil.

5. If using filo pastry, lay out one sheet of pastry at a time on the work surface. Fold to make a square and then fill and roll as above.

6. Stand the tin on a baking tray, brush with egg, and sprinkle with half the cinnamon. Bake for about 40 minutes until crisp and golden.

7. Cool for 10 minutes and then carefully remove from the tin and transfer to a heatproof serving plate. Dust the top with remaining confectioner's sugar and cinnamon. Best served warm.

LOVING SPOONFUL PUFFS

Serves: 4   Preparation: 35 minutes plus cooling   Cooking: 55 minutes

---

A variation on the vol au vent which can be filled with sweet and savory fillings. A petal- or flower-shape or star-cutter also works well with this idea. Perfect for Valentine's Day or any meal for someone special.

1. Rinse the rice in a sieve under cold running water. Place in a saucepan, pour over the milk, and slowly bring to a boil. Cover with the lid propped open on a wooden spoon handle and simmer very gently for about 35 minutes, stirring occasionally, until soft and thick.

2. Remove from heat, stir in the sugar and vanilla, and leave to cool. Discard the vanilla pod and add rosewater to taste.

3. Preheat the oven to 450°F (230°C, 210°C fan oven). Lightly grease a baking tray. Divide the pastry into 4 equal pieces and roll out each piece on a lightly floured surface to just large enough to allow you to cut out a 4inch (10cm) wide heart shape.

4. Cut part of the way through the center of each using a 2¾ inch (7 cm) wide heart cutter—this will form the lid. Transfer to the baking sheet. Brush the tops with egg and bake for about 20 minutes until risen and golden brown.

5. Carefully remove the inner hearts of pastry; keep and set aside. Scoop out the soft pastry from inside to leave crisp pastry shells. Cool the cases on a wire rack.

6. To serve, spoon the rice pudding into the cases to fill them. Sprinkle with pomegranate seeds; dust the lids with confectioner's sugar and arrange the lids on top. Decorate with rose petals and serve immediately.

Ingredients

5 Tbsp. (75 g) short grain or pudding rice
1½ cup (450 ml) whole milk
¼ cup (50 g) superfine (castor) sugar
1 vanilla pod, split
approximately 1½ tsp. essence of pure rosewater.
1 quantity puff pastry
1 egg, beaten, to glaze
2 Tbsp. pomegranate seeds
1 tsp. confectioner's (icing) sugar
a few rose petals to decorate

Acknowledgments

I'd like to thank Amanda Brown for helping me with the recipe testing (and for making all that pastry for the photography sessions!) and other friends and family who have helped me out with tasting my pie creations. I'm very grateful to Rachel Bass for providing me with a selection of her lovely pie birds for some of the photos and to Ian Garlick for creating so many lovely images with my pies.

Bibliography

Colquhoun, Kate. *Taste*. Bloomsbury, 2007

Davidson, Alan. *The Oxford Companion of Food*. Oxford University Press, 1999

Good Housekeeping Cookery Book, compiled by The Good Housekeeping Institute. Ebury Press, 1983

Larousse Gastronomique. Paul Hamlyn, 1989

Mason, Laura with Catherine Brown. *Traditional Foods of Britain, An Inventory*. Prospect Books, 1999

McGee, Harold. *McGee on Food and Cooking*. Hodder and Stoughton, 2004

Ross, Robert and Scottish Meat Traders Association. *Scottish Meat Training: A Taste for Pastry—SMTA*. Perth, Scotland.

Index